WHY WE ARE HERE ON EARTH
AND **WHAT** IS OUR **TRUE PURPOSE?**

WHO
Am I?

PETER DEACON

WHY WE ARE HERE ON EARTH
AND **WHAT** IS OUR **TRUE PURPOSE?**

WHO
Am I?

MEREO
Cirencester

Published by Mereo

Mereo is an imprint of Memoirs Publishing

25 Market Place, Cirencester, Gloucestershire GL7 2NX
Tel: 01285 640485, Email: info@mereobooks.com
www.memoirspublishing.com, www.mereobooks.com

First published in England, 2013

Book jacket design Ray Lipscombe

ISBN 978-1-86151-018-1

Printed in England

See more about the author and to purchase the book go to
www.communicatingwithbasics.com

Acknowledgement

I would like to thank Pauline Lelliott for correcting my errors and helping to put the book in order.

INTRODUCTION

The purpose of this book is to help you to discover who you really are by enabling you to view your life from a different point of view, and from that viewpoint to learn ways to remove your problems so you can enjoy creating a better life here.

Before I could help you to find out who you are, I needed to take a look at my own life from childhood to now. I needed to piece together my own jigsaw puzzle of life experiences in order to show you a way to happiness. I am willing to use my experiences to help you to realise that we all do things we don't fully understand all the time, more so when we are young. It is natural for us to try things that we feel are right at the time, and then to learn from our mistakes.

Some things we did in the past may seem rather daft to us now. They might or might not have made a lot of sense at the time. All our experiences are pieces of our life's jigsaw puzzle, and some of these pieces may not fit into place or make sense to us until we are much older.

Making mistakes is an important part of our learning process. It is the only way we learn anything. I doubt if any of us arrived on Earth as experts.

So, in order to help you find your life's purpose, I need to tell you about my life experiences. This may bring to the surface a few memories of the antics you got up to yourself when you were younger.

There are many things we have the ability to do without being aware of it. I will cover a few you can try for yourself, to prove to you that you are who I say you are. This is not because I say so, it's because you know so.

Who Am I needs to be understood completely and whole heartedly. You need to feel in agreement if you really intend to change the way your life is going. So let's have some fun and get started.

.

CONTENTS

PART 1 - **WHO AM I?**

PART 2 - **WHY AM I HERE?**

PART ONE

Who am I?

It was back in 1966 when I began to wonder what life was really all about. I started wondering this when I was in town, engaged in my favourite pastime of people watching. Some people were walking fast, as if they knew where they were going, while others were in groups chatting happily, but one elderly lady really caught my eye. She was shuffling along like a zombie with an empty look on her face as if she wasn't there. This bothered me, so I kept my attention on her.

About 20 yards further on she seemed to wake up with a start, and look around to see where she was. She then turned around, started shuffling back the way she had come and went into the shop she had obviously planned on visiting.

Although I realise that there are times when we all go off into our own little world, this disturbed me, because this lady was completely unaware of her surroundings. Questions started coming into my mind. Do we all end up like this before we die, with blank looks on our faces? Why are we here anyway? What are we supposed to be doing here? Many more questions appeared along those lines, so when I got home I started analysing the sequence of events that had occurred in my life.

The part of life over which I first exerted some control began immediately after my birth, with my first breath. It was my way of saying 'I have arrived, I am here'. After that my learning process and experiences increased.

CHILDHOOD RECALLED

I realise now that the whole of life is a process of learning how we create our lives. As babies we learn how to move our bodies around. As children and young people we go to school and perhaps on to college or university to learn how we are supposed to behave in this world. But the learning doesn't stop there; throughout our working lives we learn how to do our jobs and how to adapt to the changes that affect our work, such as new technology.

Outside the workplace, the learning continues - social interactions, marriage and parenting. Even when we retire we have to learn to cope with extended leisure time and we may spend much of that time looking back at what we have done and what we feel we should or could have done. Finally we die.

Is that it? Is that all there is to this thing called life?

That way of looking at life left me with an empty feeling in my gut. The scenario just didn't feel right. If that was all life was about, it seemed a pretty pointless mission to me. I felt there had to be more to life.

But there didn't seem to be anyone out there to ask. I felt the answer had to come from beyond this world. The only thing I had been told that was outside this world was God, and that idea didn't please me either. God might tell me off for being bad, or something.

When I was in junior school my mum used to send me to Sunday school. It was there that I first came up against this God person, or thing; I wasn't really sure what he was. I was a quiet child, something of a loner, an observer in the background than an upfront kid. I enjoyed the stories about Jesus and his Disciples. I went to many different churches, Methodist, Baptist, Church of England and others, out of curiosity.

As I grew older but still in short trousers, I hung around outside a church until the service ended, knowing the vicar always came out to say goodbye to the people. When the people had gone I asked him how Jesus had managed to walk on water. Having been admonished for my cheek and sent packing, I tried again next week with another vicar: 'How did Jesus split those five fishes to feed thousands?' I put my questions to many vicars, with similar results. Those who deigned to answer told me merely that God provides, which effectively told me nothing.

If these men of God couldn't answer my questions, I thought I would try to find out for myself. One day, after Sunday school, I thought it would be interesting to try walking on water. But that might make me wet and get me into trouble at home, so I tried walking on air instead. The first couple of steps were a bit wobbly until I got the hang of it, and then my feet never touched the pavement once. I could feel myself floating; it was real and felt better than good.

Arriving home excited, I told my mum that I had been walking on air.

'So that's why you're late home for dinner is it? Been daydreaming again have you? I don't know, you're always in a daydream!'

In senior school I went right off religion when I found out that it caused too many holy wars between countries. Religion seemed to have more than one meaning. One minute we are told that God is merciful and good, then we are told we are all sinners. We are also told we will be sent to hell if we are bad.

The next bit I just couldn't get my head around. Centuries ago, we were told by the Church that God wanted us to go out to fight holy wars. God wanted us to kill other people? WOW! I didn't like that idea so I retreated back into my shell and kept myself to myself, while watching others without being judgmental.

I learned the art of becoming invisible. I used to study our teacher in school, looking at the class. I sensed what he was going to ask as he was wondering who to pick to answer a question. If I didn't want to answer it I would imagine myself invisible. It worked; I never got asked.

Even that had its drawbacks. When he wanted a volunteer for something I fancied doing, I would put my hand up, but I never got picked. Maybe I didn't materialise quickly enough, or maybe I just didn't know how to project myself to be noticed.

I couldn't find anything in my past to help me, so how would I solve this problem? Where could I look for the truth of life, now that the Church's idea of God was off my list?

WHERE CAN I FIND THE TRUTH ABOUT LIFE?

I was still asking myself this question 30 years later. I bought the first issues of a new magazine called 'Man, Myth and Magic', hoping to find the answer there, and finished up with three volumes of the thing. I scoffed at most of it, thinking it ridiculous. But I did wonder whether myths were really ancient truths we no longer understood. Had we lost track of why the ancients believed in what they did? I felt there was more to discover along those lines, but not right now as I was on a mission to discover the truth about life.

I bought books on gemstones, astrology, colour therapy, acupuncture, runes, numerology, Yi Jing and anything else that seemed weird to me at the time. One book I read did have an interesting subject, but I can't remember its title. Most of it seemed to me to be rubbish. How anyone could expect people to believe that stuff I just didn't know.

One exercise even suggested creating your own aeroplane and flying around outside! I mean, how daft is that? Yet something in me wouldn't let the little plane idea go, so I thought I might as well try it, just to prove to myself how stupid it was.

MY LITTLE AEROPLANE

So I'm lying down on my bed as instructed, imagining the little plane and myself climbing in to it. Even now I'm thinking this is stupid, but we'll give it a try. A voice in my head says: 'Just do it'. I can see the sea from my window, so perhaps I'll go for a tour along the beach in my little plane to see if anyone is night fishing. But what if the plane breaks down and I can't get back home? What if the wind pushes me off course? What if I get lost?

No, too many 'what ifs' here. I'm beginning to feel *fear*. I think something less scary is in order. I know! I'll tour my three-storey house instead, just to see if I can fly this thing properly. That's a much better idea, I feel quite comfortable again now.

Wow! This little plane is so easy to fly. I fly down to the kitchen, straight through a closed door. How did I do that? I never even thought about opening it! This is fun, zooming round the kitchen, back through the living room and on into the spare room. I am feeling *a boost in energy*, this is great fun!

Let's go upstairs. I can go fast. I can go slowly. I can even hover like a helicopter. I have absolute control over this little plane. I like this.

Now I'm on the top landing, moving to a corner of the ceiling. What are those three dots doing there? They are an equal distance apart, like an upside-down triangle. That's unusual, three pin holes! Never seen them before!

I fly around the top rooms, then back down to my bedroom again, gently landing my plane beside my relaxed body. Just as I had imagined myself climbing into the plane, now I climb out and get back into my body, where I lie chewing over what has just happened. It feels good, and my energies are buzzing.

Then my normal self kicks back in. No, I must have imagined it all. I just pretended I was flying. It never really happened. I just put it all there myself. Anyone can pretend they are Peter Pan. I went to sleep convinced that I had been kidding myself.

I was still thinking about that stupid exercise when I woke up. While having breakfast I decided to prove it was rubbish by looking for those three pin holes which made an upside-down equilateral triangle on the top landing, so I ran upstairs. I couldn't see anything in the top corner. I was right - I had made it all up.

Even then I couldn't leave it alone, so I ran back downstairs, into the yard and dragged in a heavy wooden three-section ladder. I carted it up the stairs to the top landing, put it up against the wall and climbed to the ceiling. Looking closely, I couldn't believe my eyes. It simply could not be true! Right in the top left corner on the wall were three pin pricks an equal distance apart, forming an upside-down triangle.

I felt my face turn whiter than the wall, and I couldn't get off that ladder quick enough. I was burbling nonsense, trying to say five things at once.

That's impossible. Who saw those spots? I was on my bed asking myself these questions. *You imagined it!* I told myself. *No, you saw them,* Another voice told me. What was going on?

I picked up the book and chucked it into a corner of the room; I couldn't get out of the house fast enough. I was scared out of my wits.

When I walked through the door at work my boss said, 'You look as if you have just seen a ghost, do you feel all right? I think you'd better go home.'

Home was the last place I wanted to be right then. 'Just give me lots of work and I'll be all right' I said.

It took me about three weeks to pluck up the courage to pick that book up again. All that time I was deep in thought. I had asked what life is about and then run a mile from the first extraordinary thing that had happened to me.

That experience had well and truly thrown me out of my comfort zone. I suddenly realised how big my ego was. It had taken something bigger than my ego to knock me off the perch I didn't know I was on. I can laugh at it now, but it wasn't funny at the time.

It was slowly dawning on me that we humans must be more than just bodies. I still wasn't wholly convinced, but I knew that something big was happening, or had just happened. My bravado had vanished overnight. Now I was nothing but a big question mark, too scared to ask another question.

For some unknown reason I had a desire to push this astral travel thing a bit further. I felt there was more to learn from this experience.

MORE CHILDHOOD RECALLS

But a childhood nightmare held me back at this time. I remember that as a child, whenever I began to drift off to sleep I would feel myself rising to the ceiling and on into the attic. On the floor of this attic were half a dozen horrible-looking little goblins with funny squeaky voices saying things I couldn't understand. I cried out, but when I told my mum about them, she just said I was having a bad dream. It took about a month before they disappeared. Most people have fairies come and visit them, so how come I got this devilish bunch?

I reflected on a later period of my childhood, when I was much bigger, though no more than a year older I reckon, because I was still in short pants. I remembered another dream I had nearly every night for about a week, about standing on a cliff scared to look over the edge in case I fell and got killed. Eventually I had the courage to stand up and look down. I conquered that fear, and wondered what it would be like to fly like a bird. Then I heard a voice saying, 'Go on, fly, fly with me'. I really wanted to do that, so I did.

I tumbled at first and was overcome with terror. 'Open your eyes, open your arms' the voice said, so I did so and I started to rise. It was terrific; I was flying, zooming, lifting and swerving all around those mountains. It felt the most natural thing to do.

I flew often after that just for the fun of it. I wonder, was it that experience that gave me the confidence to fly that little plane?

Later on I went up a ladder on top of our three-storey school and found myself on a little flat roof with a 12 inch brick wall on the end and foot-square white slabs on the top. I sat on this coping and watched the children playing in the playground until the bell rang. I wasn't scared of being that high up. I was calm and happy. But I decided not to fly this time as I wasn't supposed to be up there.

THE COURAGE TO FLY

Recalling these childhood memories gave me the courage to fly without using a plane. I flew to the beach and saw people fishing and others just walking about. I wanted proof that what I was looking at was true, so I jumped into my car and drove to the beach. There were people walking about and fishing right enough, but I didn't know if they were the same people I had seen earlier.

The next day I did the same again, but this time I noted what the people were wearing. Even then I had doubts. The colours I saw were a bit weak, but the men and women were correct. The trouble was that the time gap between flying over the beach and arriving there in my car was about 15 minutes, so I wasn't always right about the number of people on the beach who were fishing.

One day I was sitting on my roof next to the chimney stack (out of my body of course) when I saw a woman walking up the hill wearing a long red coat. I left the roof and went back into my body to look out of the window on the ground floor. There was a covered reservoir in front of our terrace of houses, and on the left was a steep hill coming up to our road. From my downstairs window I could see the people only when they were near the top of the hill.

I was looking in anticipation at the top of the hill, waiting to see if what I believed I had seen was true, when suddenly this woman in a red coat came into view. That was it. Now I believed I was doing it. I could no longer disbelieve it.

It's strange how I got interested in this. It wasn't something I really wanted to do, so what did all this mean and how did it have a bearing on the meaning of life?

GAINING KNOWLEDGE

I thought whatever or whoever it was who was doing this travelling must live in my head, so I started buying books connected with the mind. I fell into my old habit of disagreeing with most of what I was reading. Those mind books seemed a load of rubbish! They kept wandering off the path. They kept justifying WHY something happened instead of going to the root of the matter to find what CAUSED it to happen.

I was finding one of Sigmund Freud's books very hard going when somebody loaned me a book I just couldn't put down. For once I found that I could not disagree with what I was reading. This book felt like me. It was so real, so true and so sensible. I read it over the weekend, all 410 pages. I have never read a book so fast and retained so much knowledge in one hit.

On the Monday I returned it to its rightful owner, wondering to myself what would be next. There had to be more than just this one book.

There was. There was much more.

COURSE TIME

On the 23rd January 1970 I was introduced to a person who ran evening courses on the book's subject. As a test run, the instructor connected me to a device which supposedly registered the negative energies we carry around in our minds. I was then asked to put my attention to something that I thought was a problem to me.

The instant I found something, I saw and heard the needle of this machine slam hard over to the right, where it stayed. The wife of the instructor frantically twisted knobs on the device to bring the needle back into the centre of the dial.

I was impressed. I hadn't realised that my problem was such a big issue to me but now, having accepted that it was, I was greatly relieved. It was as if the problem had suddenly vanished, leaving the needle on the device floating aimlessly. All this happened in a matter of seconds, with no words being spoken. It felt as if I had just blown a great load of unwanted rubbish out of my mind.

The instructor then said 'You have released that problem'. His words came after I knew I had done just that. That demonstration was the proof I needed. I knew I was on to something powerful, a place where I would get my questions answered.

I signed up there and then and completed a series of courses over a period of six or seven years. The courses led me to understand the components of the mind and how they worked, providing me with personal proof all the way. I recognised that, in reality, I was some kind of spirit occupying my body. I knew then that the energies I held in my mind, my imagination, my thoughts and beliefs were actually creating my life.

MORE RECALL

This brought to the surface an incident from my senior school days. I was fascinated by electricity and built a working model of a Ferris wheel at home with my Genero Set. Not only did it go round but I found a way to install lights on it. I also built an oval race track and motorised two Dinky cars to run on it. It took me months to find out how to slow the cars down; they kept flying off the tracks.

This setback was the cause of great disappointment to me, because no sooner had I solved the problem than Scalextric launched their first electric figure-of-eight racing track. The disappointment preyed on my mind, as this was the first time I had experienced the feeling of losing something. It left me feeling empty and annoyed, so I ditched my project. I now know what was going on in my mind at the time.

Energy has always fascinated me. We cannot see it, yet we can feel and see its effects. It creates the sort of tangible result I insist on. It had given me physical proof that it does what it ought to do. No wonder I became an electrician.

But then, wanting to know more about energy, I turned towards electronics. I was amazed when I realised that everything you see on a computer screen depends on which switches are turned on or off. A combination of switches lights one pixel, which is a little dot on the screen. It takes many switches and many pixels just to create the letter 'I'.

I wondered if our bodies worked like a computer. I wondered if our thoughts, feelings, beliefs and imagination were just different energy circuits. I wondered whether there were different switches in my body which somehow turn on and off at will and under my direction. As usual when I start thinking, daydreaming or following a particular train of thought, I ended up with more questions than answers.

My fundamental question at this stage was: 'Who am I?'

It is not a particularly original question, but it is certainly difficult to answer and explain in a way that can be grasped. I shall do my best to keep it simple.

Most answers contain words like body, mind and brain. It is as if these were essential components of this 'I'. The problem here is that we refer to these components as possessions; we say things like 'I have a … (body, mind, a brain)'. If these statements are true then none of these components can be 'I', for I cannot *be* that which I *have*.

A lot of us believe that we are not our bodies or our minds, so we can truthfully say that we *have* these two elements. Most of us at this stage settle for the 'I' as having a soul, but if this is the case, if the 'I' has a 'soul', then I cannot *be* the soul because again, I cannot *be* that which I *have*.

FINDING AN ANSWER

In trying to find an answer I followed what has becoming my usual practice of closing my eyes, looked up into empty space and asking for someone to please give me an answer. Within a few seconds a hazy movie started rolling and these images came into my mind. Little did I know then that this was to be my way into the spirit realms.

WHO IS THIS 'I'?

Imagine this world as our playground. It is the stage where we play our part in life. If you (the 'I' in this argument) have a soul, then your soul is on the stage playing its part and you are watching how your soul is creating its life. Now, if you are watching this play, then you must be in the audience. You cannot be on the stage at the same time as your soul. So does your soul know who you are - or are you just a no-body to it?

But you would argue that I have got it all wrong. 'That is my soul on stage playing its part in life. Isn't it doing well?' you might say. What's going on here? Now I am going daft.

You are in the audience watching your soul living its life on stage. Are you connected to this soul in some way? If yes, how? Watching your soul performing on stage is no different from watching your child performing in a play. I can see how you might feel proud the way your child is acting, but your child is acting out its own life its own way, trying to do its own thing, even though you gave birth to it.

How did you get into the body in the first place? Did you help this soul thing to build the body you are in? Who connected you to the soul? Who made your connection? This line of thought only creates more unanswerable questions, questions which just do my head in.

Everybody has an ego and Ego has a strong desire to want everything. So am I the ego who wanted a soul just to be like everyone else? Yes - that makes a bit more sense to me now.

So 'I have a soul' is a truth conditional upon the 'I' being Ego. And we must be living our life as ego-beings, not as soul beings.

I am still not entirely comfortable with this way of thinking. Something still isn't fitting right. It seems somehow contrived. So let's try another approach and go right back to the very beginning, to the very basics, and find out whom or what is God.

MY IMAGINED STORY OF GOD

In the beginning God looked out on his/its domain and saw nothing, so he/it decided to create its own body of energy, the thing we call the universe. On the outer edge of this universe

God created a planet called Earth. We only need to keep our attention on planet Earth to find out who we really are.

On Earth God created everything, using its energy of love and including energies that are opposite to itself. These opposing so-called dark energies have the same power and strength as God's white light energy, called love. When we put our attention to spiritual matters (or the heavenly universe), it creates an uplifting feeling in our physical body. And when we put our attention to Earth matters it often creates a pulling-down feeling, like a slight sadness, that does not feel so good.

God desires to know what it would be like to experience life on Earth, but has no desire to experience living a life here itself. If it did then there would be a strong possibility of picking up some of those dark energies, and should that happen it would no longer be pure light.

Maybe for that reason God chose never to form himself/itself into a shape that could be seen or recognised by anyone. It decided to remain pure energy without form, yet its energy can be seen and felt in everything.

CREATED IN THE IMAGE OF GOD
Imagine the following scenario:

God requested some of its energy to come forth. It wanted only those parts that would be willing to live and experience life on Earth as free beings. This way God could experience life on earth vicariously through them.

To make this happen the light of God started to grow brighter and brighter and its vibration started to vibrate more rapidly, until God shook with laughter and happiness. Sparks flew out from God in all directions. What a spectacle it must have been. All these brilliant sparks - billions of them - all assembled around this great ball of light, as if waiting for further instructions.

GOD SPEAKS

'I want to know what living life on Earth feels like, so I thank all of you from the bottom of my heart for volunteering to live and experience life on Earth for me. Each one of you is a part of me created from my energy and I am a part of each one of you. Within each of you dwells the knowledge of where you originated. I will always be with you. You are free spirits now and can create experiences on planet Earth whenever you desire to and howsoever you desire. I will gain the experience of living on Earth through each of you. Thank you.'

These spirits then started making their way towards Earth as individuals, each making its own decision. God has no intention of controlling them. They are all self-motivated and free to do as they will.

THE STORY OF SPIRIT

Let's now bring our attention to bear on just one of these spirit beings. To make it easier we will call it, appropriately enough, Spirit.

As Spirit approaches Earth, it begins to feel Earth's pull, as if Earth were trying to drag it down and suck it in.

'Wow!' said Spirit. 'This doesn't feel too good to me. It's like I'm being pulled away from God.' So Spirit digs its heels in, puts on its brakes and skids to a halt. 'There's something not quite right here' it thinks, and retreats until it no longer feel the pull of Earth's energy.

Spirit has met a problem which God well recognizes. It wants to experience Earth, but doesn't want to get tarnished by Earth's dark energy. So it sits and ponders for a while on this problem before deciding to ask God for help. God replies: 'You are a God in your own right, so you have the power to do anything. You have the ability to make up your own mind and follow your own choices - you are a free Spirit. Whichever way you choose to handle this situation will please me. Everything you choose to do is perfect for me.'

Then God sends Spirit a movie picture showing how it was born. 'I can do that,' Spirit says, so it shakes itself, and a single spark appears. Spirit is pleased with this achievement and God is also pleased. Then Spirit says to this new Spirit: 'Hold on! Stop the story for a minute! What can I call this new spirit that is actually going to live on Earth?'

A picture formed in my mind at this point of Jesus sitting on a rock waving his arms about talking to a crowd of people. I couldn't hear anything, so I decided to turn the volume up a bit, and I caught the words 'God the Father, God the Son, and God the Holy Ghost'. He kept repeating those words. Then the picture faded, but those words, Father, Son, and Holy Ghost, kept running through my mind. I imagined the Holy Ghost being the universe-creator God of my story, so the Father must be the Spirit whose shaking produced the single spark that became me, the other spirit. So who is this God the Son?

Then it clicked into place. It is quite amazing what happens when I start using my body's grey matter. The answer was staring me in the face. *I* must be God the Son! And why the Son, I thought? So I looked at what children do, giving out their love, making us feel loving in turn (well, most of the time), and learning things, like how to survive and live in this world, just as I am doing. Yes, I have got it - Earth can tell us a lot if we look more closely at things.

Then another phrase kept repeating in my mind: 'We are the children of God'.

Hold on! Our body grows out of the childhood stage into an adult body. But looking at it from a spiritual point of view, nothing has changed. It's talking about our soul, not our body. We remain a child of God all our life, though Ego may have a different point of view about that. We spend the whole of our lives learning to be spiritual, learning how to show our love, learning how to respect and accept our neighbours. We all know how to say the right words, but we often create the wrong actions in backing the 'I love you' statements up. Where did I put my gun?

This leads to the inescapable conclusion that since we are learning to be spiritual we cannot, by definition, be spirits. We must be something else.

We often say 'Oh you poor soul!' to a child who is feeling unhappy, indicating that their energy is low. On the other hand, when their lives are going well, children get excited and become very energetic, jumping around all over the place. We say they are 'high spirited'. This implies they are using lots of their body's energy.

Energy in the body cannot BE energetic; it IS just energy plodding along on its wavelength. It cannot go faster than the frequency it is on. We cannot have energetic energy, but we can become energetic when we use our body's energy to make things happen faster. Got it?

I personally don't stay high-spirited for long. That feeling has a short duration in me, so I cannot be a spirit. So from this point of view I assume I must be the soul attached to my body, and the same applies to you - you must be the soul attached to your body.

This whole subject was beginning to make more sense to me now. We souls do not have names. It is our body that bears our name. We live many lifetimes on earth. On each occasion the body we use has a different name and sometimes a different sex. Each time we come here we learn to be spiritual, possibly in different areas of life. Females tend to lean more towards the feeling side of living, while males tend to lean more towards the action side. Both can become very energetic.

The end product of these lives is for us souls to be equally balanced in these two energies, so we can create all our actions with loving feelings. Hmm, I can see I have still got a long way to go. How about you?

Now let's get back to sorting out the two spirits we call God the Father and God the Son. Let's say that God the Son is you and God the Father is the one that gave birth to you. All spirits are androgynous, including you, but on Earth your human body is not; a body takes on the attributes of one of the two sexes.

God has created a game plan on Earth which we still have not fully understood. It is linked into our relationships.

I feel there is more to life on Earth than we know about. I often feel we are a part of some future project that God has in mind for us. I know we are still in the baby stage of life, because we still act the way babies act. It is a good job life is eternal, because after thousands of years, the only thing we have learned is how not to do things and the next step a baby learns is how to do things lovingly, or properly.

We are now moving into a time of learning how to do things lovingly or better. This stage of our development is to learn how to create togetherness with love.

Our history shows us that just getting on with each other and enjoying each other's company can be quite a hard thing to do.

We now need to rename our original God, the one I have already referred to as the Holy Ghost, the one whose shaking, at the beginning of all things, produced that myriad of sparks. This, I feel, is not the God with whom we souls interact. This is God The Source of All Creation so, to avoid confusion, we will call this being 'The Source of All Creation' or **Source** for short.

This is probably an area most of us still have much to learn about. I see Source as a pure energy which has created everything. I recognise the energy of Source through the feelings my physical body feels. Source is everywhere, without features or form, just being all there is, all there has been and all there will be. Source has never turned itself into an image that can be conjured up in our mind. It prefers to remain anonymous, yet it can be recognised through everything in nature as feelings of love and perfection.

The Spirit that came from the Source, whose single spark

created you, the Soul, is the God with whom you interact. This God can look like you the Soul Being in human form if you so desire, because you are in charge of your imagination. Therefore this God is the one you should logically now refer to as your God, known as your Spirit Father. I take Heaven to be in the spirit realm.

Perhaps it might be better to call God the Father our higher self. This is a truth in spirit terms. It is the place to which you the soul look up to for guidance. You do this now in exactly the same way as you did when you were a child. It was natural to look up to your parents for guidance.

I use my higher self as my entry point into the spirit realms. It is also the door keeper to this club of mine called 'my body', which is my personal universe that contains my reality of Earth life.

The last spirit name to decide upon is the spirit that came to Earth. That's me folks, the one you cannot see, the one who has no name. I have already referred to this spirit as 'Soul', so we will stop at that. Now don't you dare say 'Poor soul, he's out of his mind' even if the last bit is a truth.

And another very important thing is: try not to say to a person 'You are Soul'. It is much safer, and sounds much more pleasant to include the definite article: 'You are **the** Soul.' Otherwise there is a strong possibility that someone in your crowd will grab hold of the wrong meaning. Remember, you are supposed to be talking lovingly to people.

I must admit, I slip up at times when talking to groups of people. I forewarn them about the mistake, so when I hear tittering going on I know I slipped up. That turns the embarrassing situation into a joke.

Now that we have renamed all the spirits, let's take another look at the new trinity we have here:

Source, the source of all creation.

This equates with the idea of the Holy Ghost.

Our Higher Self, HS for short.

Your HS is in direct communication with you and Source. This equates with the idea of God the Father

Soul. This is God the Son, ourselves. We left the domain of our personal HS at the time of conception.

Since you cannot be that which you have, you definitely do not *have* a soul because you *are* the Soul.

If you still think you *have* a soul, then you haven't realised who you really are.

If this doesn't make sense to you, it may take a bit of deep thinking on your part to sort out what you are misunderstanding.

If this feels a truth for you, then we can press on.

If you can accept the fact that you *are* the Soul Being, in your body, then it will be much easier for you to recognize all the other powers you have.

You, Soul, have a body. And your body has a 'brain' with a 'memory mind' of its own.

That doesn't mean your body does things on its own, though sometimes you might think it does. You, Soul, know that none of these things *are* you. They are just things *YOU* are in charge of and put to use.

THE STORY OF SOUL

Soul is a unit of energy, created from the energy of HS (Higher Self), who in turn was created from the energy of Source. There is no difference between these energies; the only difference is in the way you use your personal energy to create experiences on Earth.

A brief stock-take so far:

Source: The Source of All Creation. This equates with the idea of the Holy Ghost.

HS: Your Higher Self. This equates with the idea of God the Father, who is in direct communication with you, the Soul, and with Source.

Soul: This is YOU, the child or Son of God. You are the master of your own universe, which is your Earth body only.

You need to understand and agree with this first chapter if you really want to change the way your life is going. If you cannot fully accept you are the Soul operating your body at this moment in time, then *pretend* you are. The exercises further on will work just as well.

Or if all this is too much for you to grasp, then I suggest you re-read this chapter. There may be a few things you haven't fully understood. Find where or what is creating your blocks. Normally it is attached to some fear you are holding on to.

If you disbelieve chapter 1, the choice is always yours, so you may still choose to believe that YOU have a SOUL, and the cart will remain before the horse. From here on in no knowledge will be gained or understood from the pages of this book. I know there are many ways to live life, so I wish you all the best in following or finding a way that suits your belief.

There are many drastic changes taking place on Earth, and some have started already. These changes will continue for the rest of your life and for future generations.

PART TWO

Why am I here?

〜∽〰∾〜

In the very beginning we agreed to experience life on Earth, so Source would know through our experiences what it is like to live on Earth.

We as Souls are the children of Source, and Earth is our nursery or playground. Being a part of Source is the only thing we know, so we are trying to be like God, or godlike.

When we first arrived on Earth many lifetimes ago, we knew nothing about living in harmony. We just wanted to create experiences and hoped that Source would think we were good at it. We felt we had to earn our right to be a god on Earth.

Unfortunately we were not every good at creating experiences using a body. Our body wanted to follow its natural animal instincts, as it knew no other master. We are the intruders and we sensed the pain our animal body was feeling when we made it do actions different to its nature. Through our lack of knowledge we often damaged it, or hurt it in some way.

We quickly learned why Source put opposing energies to itself on Earth. These so called *Dark Energies* were not really dark; they were telling us to learn other ways, to do things that would be less painful to our body. Yes, that's fine! But we don't know what to do or how to do it.

PISCES

Source positioned Pisces in the sky so its energies can give us lessons to learn.

Pisces shows two fishes facing opposite ways. This was saying that we must create our experiences using our imagination first (fish facing one way), then bring that imagined movie down to earth and create it using our body (fish facing the other way). This allows us to see the pitfalls and solve the problems by using our *imagination* first, before we actually create our earth experience.

It was also saying: Be *Aware* of all that is going on in your space. Be aware of all that is in front of you, behind you, above you and below you. In other words, stay in the *Present Time*.

We never understood that message. We *thought* it meant to swim away from each other. For the whole reign of Pisces our lives seems to be built around separating. I feel it was really saying 'Please don't live life this way, it will be painful if you do', but we did so anyway.

Pisces reminded me of learning to ride a bike. You fall off once and after that painful experience you soon learn how to keep your balance.

Source installed on Earth, opposite energies to itself, so our body feels pain when we create experiences without using our *ability to think*.

This logic is difficult to fully understand if we don't know who we are.

Let's move along our time track to the time when we formed clans or gangs. We found that some people agreed with our way of living and we formed communities with them. Those who didn't like or refused to follow our way of living we classed as our enemies. We had an attitude of 'There is only our way'.

We didn't have television in those days to distract our attention, so we arranged mass fights to remove the enemy from our space. Unfortunately a lot of our friends were killed, and we didn't like that. Some of us moved away from the fighting game with a desire to create *Harmony*.

Let's move forward again on our time line to World War II. We are still at it; we are still fighting our so-called enemy, but now World Control, not World Freedom, seems to come to the fore. We have learned how to build massive energy bombs which can blow Planet Earth to bits. Yes we have become very powerful and clever in using our destructive way of living, though some wanted to make progress in a loving, humane manner.

Over 2000 years have passed since Moses brought the Ten Commandments to our attention, and we haven't learned or applied even one of those lessons yet. We have received gentle nudges through the ages and chosen to ignore them. I mean it shows just how backward we are! Saying that, over the past few hundred years we have become adventurous and learned how to build industries and trade our goods with other countries, but our leaders still enjoy a good war as long as it doesn't involve them personally.

Our leaders panicked when they realised the power of their atomic bombs and organised meetings with their enemies to discuss the matter. So we do know peaceful ways to solve problems. This came about after our scientists became aware of a new kind of electrical energy we call 'Electronics'. This led us into the push-button age, which looked a bit like robot warfare - highly dangerous.

Since the disasters of WWII, there have been millions of humans wanting world peace and a complete change in our way of life. Even in peaceful times we still attack nature and the Earth we live on with our modern technology. People all over the world are praying to their gods or to the sky for help. They are fed up with our destructive way of living, with no compassion for humans or our planet.

Take a good look at your life. Do you *feel* it is working perfectly? Or do things not work the way you want them to?

There is a good reason for this. Before we can know that reason we need to look more closely at our own universe, at how our body is constructed. Then we will know what tools we have, and how these tools work for us.

Source has not given us its knowledge and we do not have its awareness. But it does allow us to tap into its data banks so we can gain our own awareness of things. This is done by using a much finer form of electrical energy we call 'Quantum Energy', which our scientists are now learning more about.

Our scientists are getting closer to the basics of our body energy, but will they use it for the benefit of humans or will they find ways to abuse its power?

PART TWO

AWARENESS AND THINKING

Awareness is an unusual energy which belongs to you alone. If you glanced at a dog, nobody knows you did it. Nobody can tap into your awareness and know you just saw a dog. Neither can they tap into your mind's energy and know what you are thinking. Thinking is becoming aware of something. It gives your life a purpose. It creates your personal reality concerning the world, and those things you would like to create or experience on earth. Thinking and becoming aware are the first two energies we use to create our chosen life actions.

After our body is born, we needed to find out how we can put our pre-planned desires into action.

This knocks on the head the belief that God does everything for us. That's just our ego wanting to living a lazy life, being waited on hand and foot, because we cannot be bothered to do things for ourselves, other than to watch the telly.

HOW DID WE GET HERE?

You personally planned an Earth trip with your High Self and then you arrived on Earth to carry out that mission. The timing of the birth of your body coincided with the energies of the stars.

AN IMAGINARY SCENARIO:

You, Soul, wanted to come to earth to create an experience, and you were thinking about the things you would like to create when you got here. You discussed these matters with your HS, and the two of you sorted out the details. There are lot of details you forgot to include in your original plan. Well, we are only kids; we are only learners. Children do not think of everything in detail.

So let's say you, Soul, have a desire to be the best downhill skier in the world. So you need to find the best place on Earth to live in order to fulfil that desire. Then you need to find who you feel will be the best parents to help you to achieve that mission. You may need to find a father who already knows how to ski and who is willing to teach you the skill. Of course he must earn sufficient money to pay for your equipment and support your training. You may choose a mother who encourages you to do your own thing, although sometimes we choose one parent who is opposite to us, just so we can learn not to be like them. This parent's energy will send us in the opposite direction at great speed. We should still love them to bits of course, and we should also thank them for continually reminding us not to be like them. But sometimes we don't think along those lines, we don't thank them. Sometimes we only complain about them.

After we have been a member of this family for a while, we forget why we chose them as our parents.

Does this little scenario give you an idea on the way we plan our lives prior to arrival? Does it bring memories or feelings to the surface about your early life? Is there any animosity you feel towards your parents, brothers or sisters? If so, remember the whole family was constructed the way it is before you all came to Earth. Your brothers and sisters were your friends in the spirit realm. Before coming to Earth, you concocted many games among yourselves to play when you arrived here, the same way a group of children will invent a game to play on earth. Now you have arrived on Earth, you each play your roles as agreed in spirit land.

See if you can fathom out why members of your family have behaved the way they do, or did. What were they trying to teach you? What was it you needed to learn from their antics? Make an attempt to put any bad feeling to right. With love is better than with hate. Remember you are also playing your part in their game of life. I wonder what it is you needed to teach some of your family members and friends in this lifetime.

PRIOR TO ARRIVAL

Now I am moving into an area which is none too clear. There is a chicken and egg situation here. Which way does it really work? Does Soul have the power while still with HS to communicate with Earth beings, including their future mum, or must all communication wait until Soul arrives on Earth? I would argue that we can communicate from the spirit realm with our future parent.

I remember working with a woman and as we spoke, seeing a pinkish colour or glow appearing around her lower legs. No, I wasn't gawking at her ankles. Eventually I couldn't resist asking her if she had a daughter. She replied that she did not. I told her that there seemed to be a little girl waiting to join her family.

That information did not come from me. It felt as if someone spoke through me, but who was it?

The woman then said another person had told her the

same thing some time back. A few years later she had a daughter.

This was not the first time a strong urge to say something I knew nothing about had happened to me. I have no interest in predicting energies available in a person's future. I do not dispute that some people use their ability to tell us what energies are connected to our future. So did that unborn Soul have the power and ability to use me to talk to her future mum?

This little Soul had to hang around a bit longer before her dream of coming to earth came true. I give her ten out of ten for trying and for using more than one human to get her message across.

THE DESCENT

So let's go to the time you arrived in your mother's womb. You planned this mission prior to arrival with the help of your personal Higher Self. You left the space of your HS at the time of conception. You had a scroll of paper in your hand with all the instructions and things you intended to do in this lifetime. As you jumped into your mother's womb, your HS took the scroll of paper out of your hand, saying 'I will always be with you'. Sounds a bit like Star Wars, doesn't it?

Not until your body was formed did you have anything to work with, but you still had a lot to do. After the 'big bang' called conception, a cell divided and started forming your body. That original cell passed on all the gene information of both your parents, and the past life information you came down with, in other words your suitcase full of personal goodies. All this information was injected into the new cells. That also included your personal plans for being here. As your body was forming, each cell took notes and recorded all that was going on in your inner universe (your body) at the time, as well as all that was happening around your personal space in the outside world called Earth.

When your left brain was formed it linked up to your computer; I forgot to mention that you also brought your computer down with you. All the information your cells had been recording was downloaded into your left brain when it was complete. This is where you installed your computer; then your left brain sent all this information into your left mind, which we know as the aura round your body. You were, and still are, thirsty for knowledge. You want to know what is going on all the time. This helps to create your built-in survival system. Your left mind continually stores all information concerning your inner body activities and the outside world from the space around your body every millisecond of your life. Your cells have the ability to pick up the energy vibrations of voices, sounds, objects and atmospheres that are in your body's space.

The language you learn to speak was set in motion while your body was still being formed in your mother's womb. The speech vibrations the cells in your body sensed went directly into your left brain, ready to be used later. You may even have learned some of the food you later came to like, picked up from your mother's eating habits.

IT'S TIME TO CREATE

The first thing to be created is our physical body. We don't actually build our body, but we do supervise its construction to ensure that its shape and size matches our specifications to suit our purpose for being here.

BODY BUILDING WITH EGO

When you arrived in your mother's body, you brought your computer with you; it has on it a program called Ego. Ego has been instructed to make sure your body survives until you, Soul, decide you have no further use for your body. If Ego cannot find you, it cannot follow your instruction, so an emergency programmer kicks in and reminds ego that it dies with the body. There is no continuation, no afterlife for Ego. Sorry mate. This causes Ego to go into panic mode when it finds you are not around (the reason for this will be described later).

CELL WORK (BIRTHING)

When the sperm met the egg, your Soul arrive to make up a threesome. You brought down with you your computer with a brand new ego program to build your body. Knowing what you do about Ego, that might sound a bit risky. Actually Ego hasn't the sense to build a body, so it watches its construction instead.

Your body is created and formed into its correct shape by combining three vital energies. They contain the knowledge on your dad's side of the family and how life has been for them, and the same about your mum's side of the family. At this point your Soul joins in the party by installing your personality, plus information concerning those things you intend to achieve in this life. You know - those things you planned so carefully with your HS earlier.

Some Souls arrive at such a great speed that their mothers know when they have conceived. Your arrival was stronger than lightning striking the Earth, but your energy, though more powerful than lightning, is more finely tuned and gentle in nature. Your arrival time also aligns with the planets in our solar system. Their energies are needed to help direct your life along your pre-chosen path.

HS looks in to make sure you landed safely. Then your mum's body starts forming a cell which combines the male and female information, plus all the necessary information you need for you to finish up being the right sex, right shape, right height, right features etc, plus all the other characteristics you need to have in the body you want the world to see. So the genes in this new cell have been modified to create a new programme for your personal body, which the planets are tuned into. Isn't it fantastic the way our body creates human evolution through computer programming?

Evolution is taking place here. HS says, 'OK young Soul, you're joining earth during the computer age, so make sure you take with you all the information about computers.' When this cell starts dividing it duplicates all this new information into every cell that makes up this new body. I wonder if this is why kids today know more about working computers than I do? You see, I started using a computer when we had to make our own programmes, and repaired them when they didn't work. Each new generation of children brings more advanced information. All they need to learn is how to use it on our man-made equipment – clever clogs!

This is where we bring Ego back into the game. Ego's instruction is to 'make that body survive or you're dead', so what better chance can Ego have of getting to know about the systems needed to make the body survive?

If Ego is going to make the body operate, then it might as well learn how its energy circuits work, where its muscles are and how many systems there are to keep it running properly.

When a new cell has been made, that cell starts to make notes, by recording all that is going on in its environment. Each new cell adds new information into its DNA about the body's building and growth. Every new cell formed receives its predecessor's information, so every cell in our body knows all about the way our body was created. I have heard that a body contains well over forty trillion cells, and that is all a body is made of. Bodies are just a pile of cells continuously in communication with each other. I sometimes wonder - are these the voices I hear in my head?

EGO DEFINED

E = Energy and Go means create a movement that creates a physical action.

Ego is a unit of energy in your body which actually moves your body parts to create the experiences you desire it to have on earth.

SOUL DEFINED

Your energy is the same as Higher Self's. Both of you are on the same wavelength and frequency, which I call your personal radio station, which is on the same frequency of your body. You have the ability to tune into your HS radio station and at the same time to your body's feelings and emotions. Your energy of love is much finer and more powerful than your body's energies. You do not own any heavy physical energy, so you cannot move body parts around. That is 100% the body's Ego job.

EGO'S POWER

If your body's nose itches, you, Soul, sense a discomfort attached to your body's nose, and send a message to Ego saying 'scratch my nose please.' Ego always follows your instructions; at least it does when you're there supervising, so it makes your body's arm move and makes the finger scratch the nose. Don't forget to say thank you to Ego afterwards. All this may sound daft to you at first, but that is the way we make our personal inner universes work.

Your energy as Soul is pure love. You send out what I call white light. Your beam of loving is like a non-destructive laser beam which penetrates everything. Your energy does not belong to Earth, so you cannot use it to push a car down the road.

The truth of the matter is, Ego creates all your earth actions for you by manipulating the parts of your body, so Ego should be one of your best friends on Earth. Think on that for a minute. Ego makes your body do everything you ask it to do, and more.

It is not a truth when we say 'My ego got the better of me.' We may say that when we put our attention on some disagreeable situation to which we reacted rather violently, either physically or verbally. Ego does not have the sense, knowledge or ability to work things out for itself. It only has the ability to follow commands. Ego is a no-brainer; it only knows how to follow instructions, and at times when you are not there, it follows the basic survival instruction in its own program, which ensures that your body survives while you have gone walkabout. Or should it be flyabout!

Just think about this for a moment. Ego is nothing other than a programme on the computer you brought down with you at conception.

The first part of Ego's program is to make sure your body is made according to your specifications, and that each body system contains all the energies according to the blueprint of that body parts system. Ego directs and controls the use of earth energies. Your body can only work through the use of Earth energies, and Ego has all the maps, plans and diagrams stored on its section of the computer, so it knows exactly what energies are needed to be sent, where to create an action, or heal a faulty not-at-ease (diseased) area of your body. Somebody's got to be in charge of this lot, and Ego feels it is the top dog, capable of running this energy body. The truth is, Ego is petrified of dying, so it thinks if it runs the whole body energy system itself it will stay alive forever - dimwit!

It doesn't even realise that the animal body it occupies

eventually dies, and it dies with it. Only you, Soul, live on forever. Ego knows nothing.

A FORGOTTEN LESSON

From this point on you need to view life differently from the way you normally viewed it.

This is the part of life you have never been taught in school. Maybe those beings in charge of Earth do not wish to lose control of you, maybe because you are a sinner, as Christians are taught in school.

You, Soul, are a separate entity to your body and always will be. You are a part of Source. You need a body to create your actions on Earth and you rely on your body's five senses to know how well it created the actions of your choice. You are both different types of life energy working as a team.

BORN AT LAST

Gee! I preferred entering Mum's tummy to leaving it.

After your body was born you tune into its five senses to find out what the environment you are born into is like. Everything others say and how they act is being stored in your body's cells' data banks as each cell is created ready for future use. All the thoughts and ideas expressed by those in your vicinity are meticulously stored and transferred to your left brain, then into your left mind. This is the only mind your body has.

As a baby you quickly learned that when you made a noise using your body's throat, someone came running to you. You liked that, so you practised making other sounds to see what effect they had. You were in fact creating your early Earth experience.

The first few years of your life were the time of maximum input, when your basic impressions of this world were being formed. This body, your energy machine, was rapidly growing and connecting up all its energy circuits. There are millions of circuits in our body we don't know exist. Some we have found but don't know what they are for, like the extra strands of DNA in our cells.

At the ripe old age when you're learning to crawl, you eventually learn how to move your body correctly. We were all bad drivers at first. This thing called a body had two arms and two legs, and when you moved the right arm and the right leg at the same time, your body fell over. When you moved the right arm and the left leg at the same time, your body stayed balanced. Remember Souls are used to just floating around. You quickly realised that if you weren't there controlling your body it fell over. This body when in motion needed to be controlled and kept balanced by you all the time. Some of us have forgotten that valuable piece of information.

If the people around you in your early years were having rough times, never having any money or always grumbling, then most probably that is the way you will behave when your body is fully grown, because that is the basic information your body cells have been storing. It is not only the way you were brought up by your parents that lays the foundations for your life. All this information is being saved as Video's in 3D HD and MP3 formats, all your life. It is saved in the same way as our computers store information.

BODY WORK

It is common knowledge that when we learn to drive a car the first thing we learn is what and where the important parts are, otherwise our driving will be disastrous. Now you know who you are, the same knowledge applies to driving your body around for the rest of your life.

Our important body parts are the energy links coupled via your brain to your body's systems. As each part of your body is completed, the link is made. After you learn to walk, your body is still unruly.

Watch the way children play in their first play group. As Soul beings they continue to follow their desire to do anything they like. Now is the time they learn about Earth emotions, feelings and friends. There is a teacher there to make sure things don't get out of hand. Very young children haven't been taught our Earth rules yet.

You also have somebody watching over you in the spirit realm to whom you rely on for guidance. This is the Spirit already named as your personal Higher Self, or HS for short.

All this early information has everything to do with forming your personality and your way of living. As a young child, you were unable to distinguish the relevant from the irrelevant, because you the Soul were operating from theta and delta wave energies only. This made you *feel* god-like and loving, yet your left mind, which is connected to Earth matters, works via alpha and beta energies, which inevitably filled your body with rubbish and junk information, much of which you came to accept as your beliefs simply on account of their being there.

The energies in your left-brain mind started affecting you when beta waves were introduced to your left-brain circuits. This made Earth reality more real for your body.

FALSE BELIEFS

Your life operates mostly from beliefs you accepted from unproven facts created by the good intentions of your parents and others, plus the untrue beliefs you personally created yourself from this data, and from your own now formed opinion of the world. These beliefs control your behaviour. As a result you may be thinking of doing something in a certain way, but at the back of your mind other thoughts may be directing your actions away from that idea. This puts you in a war of the world's situation; your inner personal world desires versus the outside agreed-upon world demands. You are also learning how earth's heavy energies called *Emotions* work in your body.

GROWING UP - TEEN YEARS

By the time you have reached your teens you are thinking better. You start thinking thoughts that flow with the contents of your left-brain mind. You have been brought up to believe only things that concern Earth mattered, like you must work for your living, so your attention goes on earning money, not to stay alive but to spend on whatever you like. It may have been a bit of a shock when Mum said you had to pay something for your keep now. How unfair it seemed!

As you can see, we learn everything on a gradient and our thinking ability may not have reached the point of wanting to act responsibly, or being responsible, or acting as part of a team. Maybe at that age we hadn't learned what 'Being Responsible' really meant, as it was never taught us in school.

You eventually reach the age when you want to break away from your mother's apron strings. You no longer rely on your parents for advice. Somehow your parents seem to appear to you as wicked witches. This is often a hard time for parents to live through, especially if they never taught you the meaning of the words 'love' and 'respect'.

You decide you are going it alone from now on, so you break the ties with your parents. Sometimes you do that badly because you haven't the knowhow to do it kindly. Not only that, you closed the door in your right brain when you were about six, so you have already broken your link to your spiritual parent, your Higher Self. You have blocked any knowledge from coming to you that might make the transition peaceful.

Yes, we really know how to break ties with those we love yet still need the most. We then act like little know-it-alls with big egos who actually know nothing. It may be good fun for us, but not for our parents.

I can remember my younger years. It does have its drawbacks when we lose our spiritual awareness. We no longer feel the love others are sending us. We no longer feel anything from those around us. The cells in our body only detect earthly energies of fun, fear, distrust and other pleasant animal instincts.

We never get to know what energy people are really sending us; we think it is anything other than love. Neither do we rely on the cells in our body to tell us how our bodies are feeling in general. We are no longer experiencing and creating our lives as pre-planned; we just act and respond like the fun animal the human body is. We only want to satisfy our body's desires. It goes something like this: eat, drink, party, and sex. What else is there to do in life? Not being responsible is fun (for non-thinking human animals).

The *feelings* your physical body experiences are the only way you can find out if you are living your life as a god on earth as you intended to be, or as the animal your body really is.

We call the first effects of these emotions 'teenage revolt'. They want to do something and say 'yes that makes sense to me, yes I can do that.' That is being logical, but when push comes to shove, mentally they *think* they know, but still cannot do it correctly. Sometimes you cannot put your desires or dreams into practice, either through lack of experience or because our governments have created so many rules and regulations concerning the way we are supposed to live that it becomes almost impossible to create life the way we want it to be. Maybe this is for your safety, but we don't see it that way as teenagers.

Yet we cannot blame all this on to our parents, governments or ancestors. The natural energies that were beaming down to earth until recently came from a sign in the sky called Pisces.

In chapter one, I hammered home the words 'You Soul'.

In this chapter I assume you now know who you are, so whether I say you or we, you know I am talking about you the Soul, not your mind, brain, heart, body or anything else you may have thought you were.

Get used to this fact and know that your body's eyes are reading this page. The hands of your body are holding the book, and *you* are interpreting the energies of the words into a reality you understand. *You,* Soul, decipher the images from these word pictures to understand their meaning. I hope this statement takes it out of a simple logical argument and forms it into a fact in your reality.

From a Soul's point of view, when we create something, our intention should be to do something that gives us the most pleasure, brings us the most satisfaction and also provides some form of service to others. The money we receive should be seen as an added bonus to our pleasure of creating. Giving money is a way of showing our appreciation for something we have received. It should be our boss's way of saying thank you for the service you have given.

To some people this may sound like a crazy way of looking at work and money. But if we refuse to look at money from that point of view, it shows just how far our mind's beliefs have twisted our reality of life.

With some people making money becomes their top priority, even if they hate the job they are doing. And for some people the thought of giving a service to others never enters the equation. Yes, by all means live your own life, but have some consideration for others. Be willing to help them to survive in this world as well.

We have a new constellation of stars sending energy to earth called Aquarius. The reign of Pisces has ended. The page has been turned in the book of life, and we are to learn new ways, whether we like it or not. This energy is bringing us back on to our right track.

We are all here on personal missions, which include the survival of all. This is a better way to flow with life than playing the game of survival of self only. When following the survival of self only we upset others, either physically through our actions or verbally through our communication.

Look at the computer games on the market at this time. How many of these games teach our children to live in harmony with each other, compared to those that teach them how to kill each other? Do you feel these games are teaching our children the best way to live?

BODY RESPECT

The more you know about the energy circuits in your body and how they function, the better you will be able to drive your body, maintain it and keep it alive for a long period of time. Your body needs respect. It is more than something to drag around with you so others know you are here.

Your body is a living electrical energy unit which has the capability of looking after itself most of the time. I say 'most of the time' because you are in charge of its welfare. You need to allow it to charge its battery when you know its energies are running low.

The energies you need to feed it come from good,

wholesome foods created by nature. Our latest craze for eating fast foods is like putting diesel oil into a petrol car.

FAST FOODS SLOW YOUR BODY DOWN

Fast foods stop our bodies from working properly. This causes us to make an early exit from Earth. If you love fast foods you might as well abort your mission for being here. Actually fast foods do that for you anyway, whether you like the idea or not.

Cancerous cells are partly created by filling the body with unnatural substances which it can't handle. We also fill our mind with unloving non-survival thoughts, concerning self, others and the world. This destructive activity also helps to kill the cells in our body.

Oh Sweet Aspartame I Love You.
You are creating such a sour end to the life of my body.

PLEASE TELL ME AGAIN: WHAT AM I HERE FOR?

You are here to create your own experiences and you need the help of your body. That body you have created is a wonderful thing. It has its own pharmacy. It does its own healing and it constantly repairs and balances all its energy circuits - if you allow it to, that is. And when in a relaxed safe state, it recharges its batteries.

We cannot fill a car with petrol while driving down the road because it is still in motion. Of course not, you say, that's common sense. But we also need to use our common sense when charging our body's battery with energy. We cannot charge our body's battery while thinking about or doing other things. Our thoughts and actions are still using our energy and draining our batteries.

Maybe we don't value or admire our bodies as much as we admire our cars. When a car wears out we change it and get another one, but we can't do that with a body. All we can do is repair it, to some extent, feed it and recharge its battery. To do this we don't plug something in; we unplug something, and that thing is the contents of our left mind.

There is a quick way of doing this. You need to remove the energy input of this world for a while. You must come into PT, and notice the objects in your space for a minute, just to pull yourself right into the *now*. Take a few deep belly breaths and on each outward breath relax every muscle in your body. Feel the pleasure as your body relaxes and goes limp. Now breathe normally and go into your right brain, and tune into the love energy of your HS. Now the outside world has gone. Doesn't that feel good?

WE WASTE OUR ENERGY

When we don't know who we are, we stay tuned to the things stored in our left mind, and many of those experiences are unpleasant. Things happen in our space that remind us of some past experience, and our attention is drawn to that experience by the law of attraction. Whatever we give our attention to, we attract the images and feeling of that experience. Happy experiences have been completed to our satisfaction and are now part of our awareness.

We are attracted to the unpleasant experiences in our mind because there is more for us to do with them. They are an incomplete cycle of action, uncharacteristic of our true nature. We left them with many reasons why we don't want to correct those actions.

So when we watch two people arguing, it stimulates an experience in us that we have stored. Then we once again become the effect of all the bad feelings and bad emotions in our past experience.

We are often reminded to find a pleasant solution to our incomplete issue in a loving manner. We tend to ignore that truth. Our ego says we are right and they are wrong. If we don't, or refuse to make that correction, then the energies of that experience cause the cells in certain areas of our body to feel miserable and weak. They start to lose their life energy. Pain is caused by resisting the flow of something; in this case we are resisting the flow of our love energy.

So the real purpose of this call back system is for us to solve past issues and complete our uncompleted projects or cycles of action.

We have forgotten why we are here, so we wallow in how bad life is for us. We continue to try and prove it was another's fault. We dive deeper into the shame and blame of it. This creates an anxious state in our body and these feelings stay with us if we have turned this in to one of our ongoing pet hates. This keeps our fight or flight mode in stimulation, and our self- healing mode turned off.

Sometimes something unpleasant we see causes us to think up or dream up something that we hope won't happen to us in the future. Again these thoughts come from the left mind. Again this may put us into a false fight or flight mode. We underestimate the power of our mind's triggers. We do not know which part of our body this past unpleasant scenario is going to affect.

When we get in to this 'I'm Right' frame of mind, our body uses all the energy it can muster to feed its muscles ready to physically defend our body, so it turns off the switch that creates our body's healing.

Our body *thinks* the main mission right now is to attack the enemy. It doesn't know the enemy doesn't really exist, it doesn't know it is something we are putting there and keeping there by misusing our imagination. Unfortunately we often decide to stay in this emergency state for days, weeks, months or even years. Why we choose to stay in the dark areas of life I will never understand!

Just look at it: none of this imagined experience is in your everyday living space right now. The person involved is not standing next to you right now, but we are doing your best to put them there. And we succeed in this by attracting people like that into your life. The longer we remain in this fictional fantasy world the weaker our body gets until it ends up *feeling* mentally and physically drained. Playing the imagination game backwards is enough to drive anyone mad. I know, because it drove me mad when I deliberately did it to find a solution.

If ever you find you have dropped into this negative state, you need to look at the material world, the space you are in right away, and know that none of this negativity is actually happening to you now. Know that it's all in your imagination, so create some rapid changes to your **mental outlook,** get back into this material world and do something you love doing. Create a happy experience and notice how the energies in your body change.

As a Soul Being, you have the ability to instantly turn around and look at the bright side of life. It is just as easy to do as looking at the down side. Why live in agony? The only energy that needs *changing* is where you put your **intention.** Put it on happiness.

Now that you know who you are, you can get out of any situation that doesn't fit your desired way of living. You have the ability to go out of your right brain and in to the right mind, where you can sort the problem out with your HS without getting caved in.

If your worry is connected to something you fear may happen in the future, then stop worrying about it. Worry makes the law of attraction (LoA) work in your favour. Just reverse that worry and do what you can to make your new scenario happen. Sometimes when we worrying, we are saying we haven't a clue what to do about it. Worrying is like saying 'how useless I am', or 'how useless I *feel*'. Both of these are untrue beliefs you have created about yourself.

Why do you want to follow them? I know you are much better than that, so why not play the game, use your imagination and mentally create an experience opposite to that which you believe. The healing switch in your body will turn on and put a smile back on your face and into every cell in your body: job well done.

When we forget who we are it scares us. We think this world is all there is. Yet some instinct at the back of our mind gives us the impression that somebody or something with powerful energy is in charge of our life. When we fell into the first trap, we *thought* this energy was in our left mind as this mind keeps talking to us. So we believed everything it told us. Then we looked at everyone on Earth who we may have thought was more powerful than we are. We were really looking for ways to reconnect with our HS, but our reality has got a bit confused. We wanted to know if this Earth being was our god person. This may have set in motion a crush on idols like pop singers, football stars, famous people, etc.

WE GAVE OUR POWER AWAY

We reach a point where we are no longer being Soul, or being responsible. We give our power to other humans and allow them to use us at their pleasure. We are not being Soul when we rely on other humans to tell us what to do, or how to live our lives according to their rules. We have almost stopped thinking for ourselves. I know now, some 45 years later, why I felt so bad when I watched that person in town shuffle past the shop she wanted to go into.

The person we give our power to becomes our master for the length of time we are in their physical space, or they are in our thoughts. If we *feel* we have become a victim, it may create a slight twinge of emptiness inside our belly. We *feel and believe* we no longer own our lives. We think less of our body, we misuse it, abuse it, deny it rest, over or underfeed it, over or underwork it. We feel we are only here to satisfy the needs of others. We stop listening to our body's painful cries for help. We act the way animals act; we stay alert and live in fear, wondering what will get us out of this mess.

In this day and age it appears to be MORE MONEY. So we *think* that money will solve our problem.

When we go down that road of following others, we are no longer in charge of our lives. When we no longer think for ourselves, we find excuses to blame everyone or anyone for the things that go wrong in our lives. We blame anyone who we think is blocking our money survival line. We put so much stuff on 'pay later' systems that it puts us in fear just to think about it. We happily put chains around our neck that others control. We may even blame our Ego for doing all this to us.

We have forgotten something that's very important. We have forgotten we created our body for a very special purpose which is different to the way we are now using it. We came here on a mission and only our body can create that mission. We came here to create life our way.

It seems we need to find some way to make friends with this thing call Ego. We know it's only following a desire to survive. We have arrived now, yet we believe that 'Ego has no intention of listening to us'. This belief we created causes us lots of problems.

Source knew this might happen long before we created our first earth body, so it created a special place in the spirit realm where we as Soul Beings (with big egos) can talk with our own personal **Guidance Councillors**. I have already introduced you to this spirit. It is of course your personal Higher Self, HS for short. HS is the one that gave birth to you as a Soul Being way back in space time. Your HS acts more as an advisor than a teacher. Every spirit in the spirit realm knows that each one of us Souls down here on earth is a mini god in full control of his or her own personal universe.

Your personal universe is not earth; your personal universe is your body. Your universe does not extend any further than that. And no true spirit will ever break that rule by telling you how you should or should not live your life. No true spirit wants to control you, not even Source. Remember: Source gave you the freedom to BE YOURSELF in the first place.

YOU AND YOUR BODY BOTH NEED EGO

Ego is your 'Action Man'. Ego follows your instructions and makes your body create physical actions. It also relies on the feelings your cells send out at the time. If your cells are feeling tired, they ask for the action to stop, if they feel full of life, they ask for it to continue. We all should listen more closely to our body's desires.

We say our ego desires take top priority. We say that creating ego's desire overrules our body's requests. We as soul beings are trying to offload our responsibilities on to our poor old egos. Your life will never work properly by following that route.

However please do not expect ego to think about what it is doing, it can't. It only knows how to follow your instructions and sometimes it follows the *feelings* your cells are having. Ego only has the ability to reacts to things. When you are not there it panics and is afraid of losing its life. There is more about you not being there later on.

To know how the whole system works, you need to learn something about this wonderful thing you have created called your body.

CELL WORK (OUR MINI UNIVERSE)

Understand this well to know the cause of most dis-ease.

Your body is a miniature universe like the one we see in the sky. It is a microcosm of the macrocosm. Your body is a wonderful sensing machine. All cells, both inside your body and on the skin surface, receive and send messages. They receive and transmit information to and from each other, and the skin cells transmit and receive information to and from all objects in their outside space; this is the way your body becomes aware of the outside world. It then checks on the information stored in its mind to test the feeling about the type of people and objects it senses. It is then up to you, the Soul Being, to check on those feelings, so you know if you are in a safe or dangerous place for your body.

When we don't know who we are we create strange opinions about our bodies, all set up by the beliefs we have created and stored in our minds. They range from respect or dislike to hate or worship. It is usually the outer covering of our body that we direct these remarks to. We try to make our body look more attractive than we think it is by dressing it up. There we go, looking at the negative side again. But really, every part of the body is a work of art, inside as well as out. This may not sound like a very romantic statement to those people who *think* they only have a face. Never mind.

Your body has always spoken out, but often there was nobody to listen.

Inside your body the cells have formed into groups – a knee group, a hand group etc. These groups are able to tell you through their collective vibration if they are feeling happy or sad about what they are or were being asked to do. In plain language, it is your body's cell groups which speak up and tell you where the pain is in your body. Or they may tell you who is being a pain in the neck in your space!

As Soul, you only know about an energy called love, so you need your body to tell you about earth's energies, and you get to learn these through your body's feelings.

Now that you know who you are, it will be much easier for you to get into the driving seat and take responsibility for the body you are driving. Only in that position are you able to become aware of the multitude of communications that are going on all the time.

You have the ability to tune into your body right now and find out how its cell groups are feeling. You can find out how they felt about any action you asked them to perform in the past, and any you are asking them to perform right now. You can even sense their feelings about any action you intend to take in the near future.

The vibrations you receive back from your cells, we call *emotions:* An emotion is an earth **Energy** in **Motion**. Another way of looking at it is: cells either feel good about doing something, or they don't. Your body either wants to do that thing, or it doesn't. (Please do not use the words **energetics** or **energetic** in connection with emotions, these two words seem to be well misunderstood in our modern day language).

PART TWO

ENERGETICS

This word has been included in the English language to throw confusion into understanding energy. There are people out there who do not want us to know how life works. They may lose control of us if we learn the truth. There is no definition for this word in the English dictionary - it means NOTHING.

Understand the way energy works and what energetic means. But using the word 'energetics' has me baffled. 'Our energetics' - what does that mean? I cannot find it in the English dictionary, but it's a lovely word to say. It may be a word someone invented to give others the impression they know what they are talking about, but do they? It throws me in confusion. Please define - I like simplicity not complicacity. Eek! Is that a word or have I just invented one? It sounds good, doesn't it?

Your body may become energetic when creating some of your actions. That means your body moves about quite fast, but energy itself cannot become energetic, unless you know how to make your telly jump about on its stand, or speed the pictures up without pressing fast forward. Only you, the mover of energies, can become energetic. Think about that for a while.

WHAT MAKES OUR CELLS FEEL GOOD OR BAD?

To answer that question we need to look at another area of the body's energy. I often say that everything comes in threes and here 'Soul' has three universes to work with. As a Soul being you visit three different areas of energy: **the Past, the present and the future.**

58

OUR MIND IS ALL ABOUT OUR PAST

This mind has been created by our left brain where all our past experiences are stored, including our screwed-up creations. You know - those things we never quite got right, or never quite got finished.

Every millisecond, every cell in our body stores information using over 52 preceptors into itself. Our left brain has built an energy bubble around the body and deposits a copy of all this information into that bubble. I call this your **aura**, your '**left mind**' or your mind.

The left brain stores all our cells' past experiences in this mind. It is the only mind we have. Every cell in our body sends its information into it.

We can view any part of our life and see it as a movie, made up of images and feelings. What we see are truths, but the interpretation our feelings offer is our reality at the time of the event. Our reality may not be in line with the truth. Unfortunately we go into that mind many times a day.

When we put our attention on a past painful experience its energies cause us to feel pain in this present moment.

OUR MATERIAL WORLD EARTH IS MADE UP OF OUR PAST AND OUR PRESENT.

This is due to Earth's unique 24-hour time system. Only in present time can we create our actions and experience living, which immediately falls into our past.

THE SPIRIT REALM IS WHERE WE PLAN AND CREATE OUR FUTURE.

Also known as our imagination, or the world of images. This is the place we go to if we want to ask a question or wish to find the best ways to create an experience without causing pain to our body or harm to others.

THE 'RIGHT MIND'

The right mind does not belong to your body; it is the **'mind of Source'**. It contains the knowledge of 'all there is' and exists in the spirit realm. You, Soul, can go to this place at any time you desire and talk with your HS.

YOUR 'LEFT MIND'

The information in your aura continually forms and re-shapes your character and builds your personality. It's the way we grow as a Soul Being. You and your body's cells both use your left mind for the purpose of viewing your past failures and screw-ups; you know, those things that didn't quite work out the way you thought they would. You and your body cells rely on the information stored in your 'Mind' approximately 95% or more of each day.

Your cells are the only entities that have the ability to feel the pain of your screwed-up experiences.

Only you (Soul), have the ability to bring the contents of a left mind experience and view it in the right mind without feeling pain from its energy.

PART TWO

PRESENT TIME (PT FOR SHORT)

This area we call 'the here and now', 'this moment in time' or 'in the zone'. It is known by many names. PT is the only time we have in which to create an experience in our life. This is the time-space where we actually feel alive and feel we are living. The time we actually live in is moments long - we call that PT. Our experience continually drifts into our past.

PRESENT TIME IS THE SHORTEST SPACE IN EARTH TIME THAT LASTS FOR EVER

OUR FUTURE

Sorry folks! You don't have a future as such; your future is still a jumble of chaotic energies in the right mind. If you haven't used your *Imagination* to create your day, then you will be at the mercy of Mother Nature, and the victim of other people's energies. If you knowingly plan your next action and carry it out then you will always be in charge of your immediate future. The distant future takes a little more time to create. They take one step at a time in the now until you have created your end product.

EXAMPLE 1

This is an exaggerated common way we often look at things to be done.

You have some holiday time coming up in a month's time,

61

and you would like to spend it in some hot country, but you 'don't have the time' to plan it. When that time arrives, what are you going to do? Just jump on any plane and find out where it takes you?

I mean the date of your holiday has arrived. Haven't you forgotten something important? Are you relying on luck, or do you believe 'God will provide'? Are you hoping you will arrive at a place you like? There is no such thing as a future until you plan what and where your future is going to be. Thank goodness there is *a place of possibilities* you can visit. I call this the 'right mind'. The right mind doesn't exist in your body, you have to go through an *imaginary* doorway in the top of your head (similar to Alice in Wonderland) to arrive at the right mind.

Go on! I dare you to do something that seems crazy to this world's way of thinking. You may not have used this door since you were about six years old, so the hinges may squeak a bit.

The planning phase is linked to your right brain, which leads you out to the right mind to an area in the spirit realm where you use your imagination and plan your future experience with the help of your higher self.

EXAMPLE 2

You have some holiday time coming up in a month, and you would like to spend it in some hot country. By using your imagination: 1 You decide where you want to go. 2 You book your transport and accommodation. 3 You put a reminder on your calendar. 4 You pack your bags. 5 You sort out spending money. 6 You go on holiday. Mission completed.

When you are not sure of the best way to create something, you can always ask your HS for assistance; HS does not give you orders but suggests different ways you may like to tackle a situation. This is commonly known as receiving *intuition* - inner tuition, or inner guidance.

You are a god on earth in your own right. Which ever option you choose to follow from those offered is perfect for you. If you find afterwards that you have chosen (from your point of view); the wrong option (hindsight is easier than foresight), then you have something to learn from the experience you have just created. Nothing is perfect. There is always something to learn from every experience we create or chose to become a part of. The learning makes you wise. It's not the knowing about something but the way we use the information that lifts us up and boosts our confidence.

WE ARE NOT HUMAN

Each one of us is a bright spark of light, a unit of glowing energy called Soul. We are here learning, while owning and using a body, how to *be humane*. We are by nature a loving, caring, gentle, compassionate, well balanced Soul doing our best to have experiences and keep our body alive and healthy at the same time.

We love using our body to create experiences. If this isn't the way your game is working out then you can always change the game you're playing. Create a new game for yourself that has more pleasing results.

Your body is an animal by nature, and at times it likes to

go back to its natural wild state. Human is the name given to our animal body. It shows in some people by the way they act, especially when they are fed up with all the prohibitions and controls forced upon them. There are times when our body feels like screaming because the demands put upon it are too many. It's also natural to scream when you're excited. Dogs howl and bark and humans laugh, scream, shout, and bawl their eyes out when they *feel* like it. Our body can do more than the other animals, that's why we chose it.

GENUS V GENIUS

Our genus, the animal side, wants to follow the natural way of its species, whereas you, Soul, the genius, wants to have experiences on Earth that please both you for awareness and your body for satisfaction. Using a body to create our experiences is a difficult thing to do when we look at it from Soul's point of view because personally we cannot move a body; our knowledge about the human body is very limited.

When we were born, we found the body to be a very slow-moving machine compared to the speed at which we move. We had to learn how to move each limb separately in a set order to keep the body balanced as we put it in motion. By using energies, like determination and desire, we eventually got it to do the things we desired like crawling and eating. Our first experiences caused our body slight pain, and the pain was there to tell us the experience we were creating was not correct.

After a few bumps and bruises we learned to crawl with less pain. It was the pain in our knees that encouraged us to learn the art of walking. We also learned that we cannot take our bodies through material objects. Since those days, learning from our experiences has not changed. During those early days we constantly spoke with our HS, who magically turned into our fairy friends to find out how to create the next experience we desired to have.

Fairies, angels, and our spiritual playmates played a big part in our early lives. We learned the hard way that it was better to follow the guidance of our Higher Self or the advice of our spiritual playmates. We found it to be less painful for our bodies.

Everything on Earth has an opposite, and you are about to meet your opposite: Sometimes we call our body the ego. I suppose that's better than calling it an animal, yet I have seen many humans acting like animals, as we all have, no doubt.

They love showing that side of us on TV. Why? Are they saying we need to be controlled? To me that is the degrading side of our nature.

Oh dear - I forgot! We have been told that we are all sinners. Maybe that's their way of saying they don't want us to forget it. Showing us movies that hint at the way we are at times gives the Earth's powers that be the right - or is it the power - to control us rowdy lot. Haven't our ancestors conned us well!

AT TIMES WE ARE MILES AWAY FROM EARTH LIFE

When we were very young, when we slept we space-travelled a lot, without taking our bodies with us. This caused no problem until the nerves in our brains were connected to the muscles in our bodies, then our bodies tried to mimic the actions we were actually creating in space and our body fell out of bed.

Not all circuits are completed in our brain at the same time; some take a lot longer to form and connect, so falling out of bed appears to us to be a creation hitch more than a learning process.

Everything you see as a soul which cannot be seen with your body's eyes does not belong to Earth. Your thoughts come through on an energy frequency especially created, so only you Soul receive them.

When your attention is on something other than that which you are doing on earth, then you have left the earth stage and gone what I call 'Walkabout'. During walkabout you are not with your body, so you leave it open to danger. Accidents happen when you are not there controlling your body.

Your body's brain translates energy into a picture format you understand. Your 'thoughts' are made of a holographic type energy we call imagination. imagination does not belong to earth. This is an ability you, Soul, possess. So as you may have already realised, you should never leave your body in motion when *thinking about something else*. It is wise to stop creating your actions in order to do your thinking.

Before you knew who you were you most probably *thought* God or your Angels were creating your life for you, or maybe you thought your ego was creating it? It always had to be someone else doing things for you. You had nothing to do because the belief you had been given by those controlling people indicated, not always in words but in thought form, that you were a nobody, and you may have taken that to mean that you did not exist as a very special Soul Being.

This belongs to Book 2, but you need to know this information now. You do not have a body. You radiate your energy the same way Source does. That is why nobody can see you or see Source. Yet you have the ability to see anything Source has created (on request only). The same applies to you. Nobody can see you, yet they can see and feel all your creations. You need a body so others know who created your masterpieces.

> *You are a marvellous soul who has come to earth to*
> *have fun with your creations.*

After you bring an *idea* down from the spirit ream, you pass this information over to your body, which actively created the experience on Earth for you. You may realise you have a few more things to learn from its outcome. Maybe the effect your masterpiece caused was not exactly what you intended. *Remember, you are a unit of love* and you don't want to go around upsetting others.

But that's not a problem; you are here to learn from your mistakes, so you correct your errors, and next time you create that experience a slightly different way, which improves the pleasure you and others gain from it.

Perfection is not possible on Earth. We always have something to learn from our experiences, so the best we can do is keep aiming for perfection, keep aiming for the best we can do until we feel satisfied and comfortable with the result we have created.

You have a rough idea how creating on earth works now. You know the things Source and HS will and will not do for you.

Have you changed your belief about 'God doing everything for you'? Come to think of it, has God ever physically done something for you? If you are being honest with yourself, the answer has to be a big resounding 'No!'

Neither Source nor HS has ever exercised control over you so you have to do their bidding. Neither have they done anything for you other than to offer you sound advice on different ways for you to create those actions about which you requested more information. Often your HS arranges for somebody to come into your space, usually an Earth being who knows about the subject you are asking about.

Anyone in the spirit realm would be in breach of contract if they did anything for you. Earth beings love changing the rules of the game to suit their way of living. With spirit beings it always remains the same way It WAS, the way it IS and the way it always WILL BE.

In the spirit realm, you are never placed in a situation where you are overwhelmed by things you do not understand. You are never the effect of something you cannot find out about. On Earth the opposite applies. You can put your body in a situation where you become overwhelmed by something you do not understand. Often your body is the effect of things you know nothing, or very little, about. Take the additives in food for example - we don't get sick for nothing, we get sick through someone else's creation, which we know little or nothing about. And that's the way they want it to be.

When you feel you have been overwhelmed, then you have been given information that is beyond your reality of understanding, beyond your level of awareness. Maybe it is something they insist you believe. Many of your beliefs come from the reverse-engineered earthbound version of living. Sometimes we have to pay some form of penalty (even death) if we don't obey their commands. Some of our Earth systems have been created to control through fear, not through love.

You make the choice to believe something. It is always in your hands.

Whatever you choose to believe is perfect for you. There is no 'this is the only way', or 'this is the right way' for anything. Some ways help us to make fewer mistakes than others, but we still have to put our thinking caps on and decide for ourselves which way we intend to go. We learn our lessons after creating the action. Only then are we able to look at our mistakes. In the movie business they scrub their 'mis-takes' out and go for another take.

If you are doing something that is making your body feel uncomfortable, then you are doing it without showing love or respect for your body. Banging your head against a wall when you're annoyed or in a rage is not going to solve your problem; if anything you're creating more problems.

Your body worships you, and follows your instructions to the last detail. If your attitude is that you have to cart this body around wherever you go, then you are not sending it love.

It knows whether you love it or not through the pain or pleasure it feels during and after the creation of the experience you asked it to create. Your body is a living, feeling machine.

WHO IS GOING TO CLEAN UP OUR MESS?

As children we were often told to tidy our room. When we looked in the room we saw no mess. Everything was there the way it was supposed to be according to our comfort level. We might move a few things around to please Mum, and that was it. When we leave, Mum tidies the room the way she wants it to be. Then we are both happy, because we have a poor memory at that age and don't remember where things are, or were.

Now let's look at this from Soul's point of view.

Earth is the playground where we act out our lives. Over time we have created a lot of mess. We have disrupted nature to the best of our ability. We have poisoned the air we breathe, polluted the water we drink, ruined the land we grow food on, killed the creatures we don't like, chopped down the forests etc. You name it we have successfully done it, to satisfy our greedy desires. We have very little consideration for Mother Nature. But if Source asked us to clean up our playground, we wouldn't see any mess.

Our mental reality as Soul Beings has only now reached the level where we are beginning to see, understand and respect the ground we walk on. We are still slightly unruly and think we know best, but in Britain we are at least taking better control of our home waste. We no longer bury all our rubbish hoping that plastic waste will grow into plastic flowers; our awareness has lifted on this matter. Maybe we were attracted to doing this by a desire to making money on the waste products. We have learned how to recycle our rubbish.

This small step leads us into other ways of cleaning up the

planet we live on. One small step at a time in the right direction allows our awareness to grow on the subject we have our attention on. Just like children who eventually learn how to make their room look tidy after they have learned what the word tidy means.

This may take us a long time, so Source has arranged for Mother Nature to send in the cleaning ladies to clean our playground up. Have you noticed a sudden glut of tsunamis, earthquakes, volcanic eruptions, tornados and sudden changes in temperature, all happening in a short space of time? All this happened after Aquarius started sending its energies to earth. The cleaning ladies are doing a good job, and we haven't a clue what is really going on. Well - we are only kids aren't we?

Maybe Source is digging the garden of Earth right now, getting rid of the rubbish we have left behind through our messy way of living.

Aquarius energy is lifting the veil, so we can get to understand the spiritual way of life more easily. The problem is, the more Aquarius shows us new healthy ways to live, the more Earth's dark energies become empowered to stop us from changing. Energy is counterbalance. If Source thinks it is time for us to move on, and desires us to lean more towards the light, then the darker side of living gets disrupted and annoyed. It resists, it kicks out stronger, it wants us to continue our old way of life. We do not have the knowledge or the knowhow to create this change on our own, so what will be will be.

Gentle chaos is reigning on earth right now, and will continue to do so until sufficient Souls have built their energy links that lead us to the correct ways to live. We insist on receiving correct guidelines this time. We want uplifting energy ways that we can all follow from now on.

Of course things will go wrong from time to time - that's our natural way to expand in life. Have you ever wondered why wars break out? Is it because we do not know how to listen to what is bothering the so-called enemy?

What is an enemy anyway? Is it someone who disagrees with us, or someone we disagree with? Do we not know how to balance things out to please all concerned without bringing power and money into the argument? I haven't a clue about these matters, I came here on a different mission, but someone knows a better way to solve problems along those lines.

Source is indicating it is time to change from our old egotistical money track interests, and get on to our true loving path. Some people may think that remark extremely funny or ridiculous. We have been heading for the pits for too long. The Aquarian era has arrived. We have cried out to the sky enough times and we desire changes to be made by the gods. See there we go again, demanding that somebody does something for us.

We have to start readying ourselves for change. Remember - nothing is going to be done for us.

Subtle energies have been arriving on Earth and in our brains which are causing us to desire change. These energies are making it easier for multitudes of people to look at subjects that will help them find a way back to being spirit minded, where they belong. They may not know this. To them they are out looking for – er, something!

The way I see it is like this: Source is making it much easier for us to accept the spirit realm as something real. Orbs have been flying around Earth and have been picked up on digital cameras. UFOs came back, and we were not as scared of them as we used to be. Since we have not heard any reports on television on how aliens are killing us faster than we are killing ourselves, we accept them as visitors to our planet. Crop circles are spinning their beautiful pictures, but the shame of it is that our mentality is so far beneath theirs that we do not understand the message they are trying to put over to us. But we love the pictures. I'm sure some people understand their message. but we do love keeping secrets don't we. Those who know need to have the courage to speak up. Keeping secrets is old hat.

To the majority of us these symbols mean nothing, so we admire and enjoy them as art instead. It is as if these highly-intelligent beings are trying to explain simple mathematics to meerkats.

If we want to change from our downward spiralling way of living, which is another way of saying we are slowly committing suicide, then the first thing we need to change is ourselves. Are these crop circles showing us ways to do that?

We cannot teach others how to get out of their personal mess if we haven't found a way out of our own. We can only teach that which we know, that which we have gained knowledge from and applied to ourselves. When we find a method that works successfully on us, then we can share it successfully with others.

We cannot teach others things we do not have a good workable knowledge about, things we do not fully understand. We cannot call that our truth. They are just learned procedures from diagrams in books etc, followed by robotic actions.

Some of the procedures I have followed lead me to no real end product to talk about. Sometimes the truth is only half grasped, so it is half taught. Some people talk a lot about nothing, then hope we get their meaning.

We need to learn from a subject we choose that excites us and use it on ourselves to make sure it can be part of our reality. If it creates a beneficial effect on us; something like 'Wowee I can feel the difference in my body right now. Fantastical!' Then make it your truth, but no pretending. Saying something is 'awesome' after listening to someone spout out a few words is saying we are easily fooled. Maybe we were only supposed to remember the awesome bits anyway.

A system becomes our truth after we have applied its cycle of actions and experienced its end result. That does not include those systems that say the magic words like 'If you do this, this will happen'. That is a controlling technique. Better words to use are 'Let's try this, then ask your client what happened'. Wow! Now your pupil is in charge of the results. They were not directed to what they were supposed to experience. This approach can be applied to both good and bad beliefs. It is better when we are forced to *think* and form our own opinion about an experience, or belief. We have to make up our own mind to see if it was real or not for us, and whether or not we want to use it in the future.

WE ARE HERE TO LEARN

Before you can learn how to get things right, you need to know how we got things wrong. So let's use communicating as an example.

When someone upsets you or makes you feel sad you should be asking yourself 'What is it I need to learn from this feeling?' You may need to follow it up with 'How do I do that?'

Before talking to yourself you need to be in the present (PT) and aware of your surroundings. You need to be here, and know you are saying those words right now. That might sound a bit daft, but it's a must do thing if you want peace of mind. You may be surprised at the number of times your attention is elsewhere when you talk to yourself.

Often you are running on automatic. When you put things on automatic you are not here. You have gone walkabout to the area where your thoughts are. This is to the experience in the past you are talking about, and that means you have gone to where your experience was.

Understand and accept the fact that you, Soul, travel faster than the speed of light when not with your body. Things continue to go on in and around your body's space that you are unaware of until an accident happens. Often no accident happens, and you drift back into your body and everything is still perfect.

Take a look at this example. You have just popped out from work, and are sitting in a café ready to drink a cup of tea. You take a sip and find it is too hot, so you sit there with the cup still in your hand as you put your attention and thoughts on something that happened at work. That means you, Soul, have left the café while your body is holding a hot cup of tea.

In ambles another customer, with glazed eyes, not sure where the counter is. He sees the counter and ambles towards it. He is dreaming and miles away, his body also on automatic.

He doesn't see your chair sticking out and bumps into it. This semi-wakes him, so he utters an automatic 'sorry' and keeps ambling towards the counter.

That bump caused your body to spill the tea over the table and into the lap of the person sitting opposite you. That jolt brought you, Soul, back in a hurry, and you're wondering what all the fuss is about. I mean, you had only gone for a second! I won't write what you said to the person who bumped you. You can use your own imagination for that. I wouldn't be surprised if the words you uttered did not contain any love in them.

Actually you were to blame for that accident. If you had stayed in PT none of this would have happened. You would have been aware, heard clearly and noticed that dreamy person walking towards your table. You would have put your cup down and shouted 'Watch where you're going', or some other choice words to prevent an accident. Being in PT prevents most of your accidents from happening.

To help you to learn from your mistakes, Source has put negative or dark energies on Earth equal in power to its own loving energy. This allows you to become aware instantly when you are doing something that is not quite right. It sends an unpleasant or uncomfortable feeling to somewhere in your body.

You as Soul cannot be harmed in any way, and you have no way of knowing if you are getting your body to do things right and moving it towards survival, or doing things wrong and moving it towards non-survival. You need to tune into the feelings your physical body is feeling to know which way you are travelling. You need to rely on your body's *feelings* to tell you if the experience you are creating right now is raising your spirit and bringing you satisfaction, or causing you to feel down-hearted. Moving the wrong way will make your body feel sad, with less energy. Continuing to follow a downward path will eventually cause your body physical discomfort and illness.

I think Source has worked this system out well. Just imagine some of the unpleasant experiences you have had. How do they make you feel right now? Doesn't that prove this to be a truth?

When you put your attention on an old experience stored in your mind, the cells that created it instantly come to life and show you the emotions attached. If that experience is not making you feel good right now, and you continue to mentally re-run through its actions, your cells will get weaker through the strong feelings of discomfort and pain. There are no other ways your body can let you know about its survival or non-survival actions.

No loving feelings come out of our left brain's mind, only hate, bitterness and verbal comments like 'I'm going to get my own back on you', or 'I feel useless' type feelings. Only wrongly created and disruptive, destructive experiences are stored in our minds.

MYTH BUSTING

Source has no intention of passing its own infallible way of doing things down to you. If it did you would be a clone of Source and there would be no game for you to play.

As I said earlier: Source has created you as a free being in your own right. Source hoped that in having this freedom, you would always remember where you came from. But you had forgotten, hadn't you? Not only had you forgotten who you are, but some of us have fallen into a lazy way of life by not thinking for ourselves.

We are all created as separate beings, and we all do our own thing. This is easily proved by watching another undertaking a simple task that you also do; whichever way they accomplish that task will have their personality attached to it. It will not be exactly the way you do it.

It is possible to act as if we are all one. This only happens when we use our animal body's herd instinct. Following our 'safety in numbers' mentality will not lead to Soul expansion. The actions resulting from thinking that way are all too apparent in this world. We clear forests, poison our drinking water and pollute the air we breathe. We use pesticides to kill off so-called pests without finding out why Source put them there. We think that we can make drugs more efficacious than the natural herbs Source has provided on earth for all life forms.

Some of us mock natural laws and degrade nature's pharmacy as rubbish; we have learned how to kill people without the need for war. To cap it all we may even add the phrase, 'It's nothing to do with me'. If you look at life honestly we have learned successfully how to get it wrong. We have learned how to live life on a downward spiral. There is no one alive on earth at this time we can blame for this, even if we do feel guilty.

Yet Source allows everything to happen the way it IS. Everything we do is still blessed by Source. Source gave us Earth as our playground, our home. Sure, we can do what we like in our own home. If we want to fill it with junk (dark energies), we can do that. If we want to turn our home into a place unfit to live in, we are free to do that as well. If at some time we get fed up with the conditions we are living in, we can always move home. We are acting like kids running amok, who have never received instructions on the way to live in harmony with each other.

I often wonder… if we wanted help with the housework, like vacuum cleaning, would Source help us by asking Mother Nature to send down the cleaning ladies? Would they use lightning and hurricanes to clean and disinfect the air? Would they send tsunamis, storms and floods to wash the floor? I am under the impression that whatever we want, if we ask Source it is always willing to help us to achieve our desire. But if we decide to rot in somebody else's brilliance, then that may be a different matter altogether. That's like saying 'Daddy has lots of money so I'm going to spend it for him'.

Most of us have a belief, even if we have buried it deep inside us, that when we have finished here we will be taken to some heavenly place beyond the stars. It doesn't matter what name we care to call living a heavenly life. Are we following an earth belief, like looking for a reward we have not earned? Well, I honestly don't know if that is a truth or not, but I am fairly certain in my *feelings* that this may not be the whole truth.

So let's look at it from another point of view.

Say you were Source, and you had planted a special brand of seeds in your garden called humans. Some grew, whiled others became very weak through lack of fertiliser (inability to receive light energy). You do everything you possibly can to energise those weak plants, but despite your effort they just refuse to tap into the light and become energised. What would you do with those almost dead plants?

If Source took them back into its body of light, then it would be like placing bad fruit in the same bowl as good fruit. We are already doing that on Earth and we know what happens - the bad ones win. So you would most probably put them on the compost heap or dig them back into the earth, as you have no further use for them.

We can't do anything with those that choose to fail. We cannot alter their power of choice, we cannot win all situations, as perfection is not possible on Earth. So maybe those Souls remain on earth and just rot, or maybe they believe Earth to be pure heaven and stay here as forms of unpleasant entities without love. Source never gives up on these beings, but what happens to them next? I don't want to know. I prefer it to remain beyond my reality.

We Souls have the ability to perceive the world of Source through our imaginations, but we need a human body to be recognized by others. We also need a human body to communicate what we see to others, and we need a human body to actually create our experiences.

By using a physical body we are able to communicate our thought and express the emotional feelings our body feels, verbally through its mouth and physically by manipulating its limbs to create the actions we desire. We do this so the love energy we are can be seen, felt and sensed by others.

It used to be our elders who were the wise ones in our lives. Since we have been living backwards, this is no longer a truth.

The words of wisdom now come from children who we have not yet corrupted. They are fresh down from the spirit ream? on missions to show us ways that will put us back on track. All we need to do is listen understand and learn. Their knowledge is simple, direct, without reservations.

DANIEL'S STORY – DO YOU KNOW JESUS?

The story is told of a three year-old boy called Daniel who was on a bus with his mum going to visit his grandma. Suddenly he got off his seat and in a loud, squeaky piercing voice asked each passenger in turn, 'Do you know Jesus?' He fixed his eyes on each person and wouldn't let them go until they gave him an answer. Then he walked back to the front of the bus and addressed them all.

'Jesus is very annoyed with you all, because you didn't understand what he was saying to you. You idolised him and built churches in his name, yet didn't follow what he taught you. I know, because I was with Jesus a little while ago and he told me so himself. He said that he was not what people were saying he was. He said he was just a man showing people a way to live.'

Daniel's mum, who was not religious, was flabbergasted and embarrassed. She had never told him about Jesus, or anything about religion. He wasn't going to school, so he couldn't have learned about Jesus from there. Where did his information come from?[1]

[1] Author's note: Daniel's story came from his mother, who is the daughter of a family I have known since 1965. I was told this story by his grandmother and it was confirmed by his mother later, round about 1989. When I decided to include the story here I tried to contact Daniel's mum, but was unable to do so. I asked his grandmother to pass this on to Daniel's mother if she heard from her daughter at any time. I often wonder if Daniel has ever been told what he said on that bus some 20 odd years ago.

Could it be that Daniel's natural ability at that age to tune into the spirit realm came into play? That would prove the spirit really is a truth. Could it be that he hadn't learned how to lie yet, that he was speaking his truth and was recently with his friend Jesus? We hear a lot of truths from young children that are different to the way we *think* things are supposed to be. We normally brush them off by saying their imagination is running away with them, but really their imagination is working perfectly and showing them truths that we no longer believe in or understand.

SOME ABILITIES YOU HAVE

You have the ability to sense the power of a person's energy when they talk. Some people project their voice six inches from their body and may be afraid somebody might hear them. This may stem from a belief created in childhood. Others talk to the people at the back of the room. They desire everyone to hear them. How proud are you to be here? How proud would you like to be?

Another example of feeling a person's energy is in their handshake. Some offer you a limp hand containing no energy, while with others their hand is vibrating with life energy, showing their confidence. How confident are you in projecting your beliefs out into the world?

We are separate individuals and I prefer to remain odd - take that which way you like. I cannot find any reason why I would want to be like somebody else. Do people try to copy others simply because they feel those people are better than them? You can always improve your skills. Feeling not good enough allows you to be controlled by others. So I prefer to stick with my well trusted game plan:

'All Souls originated from Source and became individuals.
All Souls remain connected to Source.'

We are all separate Souls, each creating our individual way of life as understood through our personal points of view. We follow our own beliefs, true or false, to make sense of the world; this forms our opinions on the reality of things. Through our personal beliefs we create our mental and material actions, and the way we create our experiences proves to us that we are different. If we were not all different, then we would not be able to find a good reason to fight among ourselves, would we?

Never blame the person who wants to kill you. Blame yourself for not finding out why they want to kill you. Sort problems out by understand life from both your points of view. Ah yes! By the way, this must be done before you attempt to kill each other.

If you did the same things all your life I'm sure you would get bored very quickly. Source knows this, and would also get bored having the same type of experiences being fed back to it from millions of Souls. This is why Source gave us the tools which allow us to be individually different. That means we have the ability to make up our own minds about everything we do, say, and see in this world.

Source has not created a one way system. Source has made sure that we all have the same energy ingredients to create life our own way by using our own supply of awareness, knowledge and determinism. Now Source will never get bored by watching a load of robots doing its will.

Source has designed us so it can enjoy watching the way we experience living. It can see all of us, all doing our own thing, trying to make life here work our way. I'm sure Source has a sense of humour and laughs at our antics, the same way we laugh at the antics of our children.

If thunder was the belly laugh of Source, I feel I would hear thunder often when Source tunes into the way I try to make life work. I am so pleased I am not supposed to be perfect.

When things are not going right for me, sometimes I grab Ego by the ear and say, 'Come here you little idiot, stop trying to live life your way, just do what I tell you.' Then I have to put my thinking cap on and talk to my HS. I ask 'which is the best way to do this'? HS shows me a few options, so I do it the way my body feels is best way to do it for me.

Ego knows that you often fly off like a bird whenever you feel like it. And at those times Ego shows its true nature; it gets very scared and doesn't know what to do. It dives into your left mind to see how you did it before. It looks at the mistakes you made and repeats them.

You will always be different from others. It is your differences that make you special, unique and therefore valuable to others.

Recognising how valuable you are to others should be exhilarating. It should thrill you to know that you are not a robot and do not have to follow the leader. You do not have to do what everyone else is doing unless that is what you choose to do, like taking part in some group activity.

You are always your own self. You are happy or sad depending on how you want to be at any time. You are alive and different. You do not have to be like someone else. Just scan through your life and find some of the unpleasant people you have met. Aren't you pleased you're not like them? See what I mean? So be grateful you are who you are!

It is wise to spend a little time looking again at the experience you have just created so you can see if there is anything you can make more perfect from your point of view next time. You always do the best you can, so praise your body for creating it that way for you. Sometimes without warning your HS says 'Your best could be better if you were to correct these little mistakes'. It then shows you a few errors, or sometimes you already know about them. So appreciate the good that comes out of a badly-created action.

With self-awareness in place, you do not degrade yourself when doing things wrong, or differently to others. There are people out there trying to find out how to do things the way you do them; it's just that you haven't met them yet so you cannot show them.

To untangle any confusion you may have about life, ask some or all of the following questions.

Are we really all one on Earth, and if so, all one what?

What is the purpose of Source giving us free will, if we are not allowed to use it?

Have we been put here solely to create the desires of Source, or did we choose to come here to do our own thing?

If we are following the desires of another, aren't we being controlled in some way? Aren't we being their slave?

If we are supposed to follow the instructions of Source to the letter, then why did Source create energies that are opposite to its self on earth?

Given the knowledge you have so far acquired, these questions should be easy to answer.

On earth we are taught how to follow other people's belief systems. If that is on a subject about which another knows more than you do, then learning from them is to your advantage. When you do as you are told regardless, then you are giving that person the power to control you.

THE BALANCE OF POWER

Your body has two brains. Your left brain is connected to everything to do with your reality of the world up to this moment in time. From this information you mentally create your own beliefs which form your state of stability on earth. It helps you to make up your mind about which way you want to travel though life.

Unfortunately this also shows what we call the Ego side of living. This is a false truth because you have already learned that ego is an idiot incapable of thinking for itself. What is really happening is that you, this highly intelligent Soul Being, have chosen to rely on and follow the contents of this mind to live your life and create your experiences. You have as good as called this mind your 'god'. This is the biggest mistake you have ever made in life.

This happens to most people. You used your body's eyes and think this is the only reality there is. You may have included an attitude of thinking that you know it all. But as you travelled down that road you met blocks and obstacles to everything you wanted to do. You are travelling on a downward spiral of energy towards the death of your body. Your abilities are becoming less, and your esteem is fading away; your confidence in living life your way is gradually disappearing. You may reach a point where your body is insisting you look elsewhere for HELP; your idea of how to make life work is not working. Be willing to accept that as your truth and be willing to change your way of living.

Do you remember the time when you were very young and gave to others the only energy you have? That was your love. You were godlike, with the intention of moving in an upward direction. You were willing to gain knowledge on how to *be* with your body. You tuned into your body's *feeling* and felt what your body thought of your efforts. When what you were doing made your body feel sad, you cried. Pain was the proof that you were moving on a downward spiral. Then you smiled and you were happy again. You realised that it is better to change direction and be happy than to stay where you are and be sad.

Remember how you joyfully agreed in the beginning to let Source know what it is like to experience life on Earth from your personal point of view, from your standpoint, from your magnificent god-likeness? It was easy to change when you were young, and is just as easy now - once you have learned how to get rid of your negative blocking beliefs.

Does all this just sound like rubbish, or just a load of fancy words? Does it sound like me stating my point of view? If so, then quieten yourself down and look into yourself and see if you can find your blocks.

THE SHOCKING TRUTH

Everything on earth is energy, and you have been taught how to live backwards. Earth is a planet of illusions held together by Earth time. Earth shows us the end products of our creations, which we look at to gain more awareness and learn from. Your material masterpieces disintegrate over a period of time. Nothing is permanent on Earth. Even the body you have created and are now using has a limited lifespan. You are eternal - you never die.

REALITY

As from now, you, Soul, need to connect with the pure energy in the source of all creation to create your future experiences. To do this you need to move away from Planet Earth and actually go to the place where Source has stored its energy. This means you have to leave your body in a safe place for a while in order to visit the spirit realms. You will meet the doorkeeper of the spirit realms, who just happens to be your personal Higher Self. No ego beings are allowed in as they would do their best to contaminate its purity. Darkness cannot penetrate the light.

Your **imagination** is the energy tool you use that leads you or takes you to reality. Imagination is more real and helpful than anything else you rely on upon this planet. Your imagination is the energy that shows you your life experiences. Nothing else is real here on Earth.

It may take a little while for this piece of knowledge to sink in. Later on it will become easier to understand how this is so and why.

LIVING WITH A BODY

Having the satisfaction of knowing who you are at last should cause a few changes in your outlook on life, and that's fine if it has already happened. If nothing has changed yet, then this is a good time to tune in to your body's feelings. Let your body talk to you, see if you need to make a few changes.

Put these questions to your body. Let its feelings provide you with the answers:

IN LIFE

- Do you want to be uplifted or downtrodden?
- Do you want to be made more of, or less of?
- Would you prefer to gain knowledge from the spirit realm, or be denied knowledge on the Earth plain?
- How does the belief 'You are a separate being' feel to you?
- Has any of this information upset your comfort zone?
- Does the belief 'You are a loving god on earth' *feel* like the truth to you?
- What do you think about Source experiencing Earth life through your creations? Does that feel good to you?
- Do you still feel you are an unknown entity, or an ego being?

The above questions are asking you to be honest and notice

how your body *feels*. You as a loving Soul being can only find Earth truths from the responses your body shows you. Your body has a range of feelings between pleasure and pain.

WHAT IS EGO'S JOB?

In the beginning, when Source created animals on earth, it created an animal called Human. This animal was no different to the rest of the animals. It roamed the world and relied on its natural instincts. It followed the directions of nature just as all animals do to find where food is to ensure survival.

There came a time when Source looked at all the animals to see how they were surviving. Source was looking for an animal to install a part of itself in, and noticed that the animal called Human had learned to use its body in more varied ways than did other animals and most importantly had learned to walk upright. So Source chose the human animal to install Soul in. Source then renamed the animal as Being Human, which we promptly renamed to Human Being. From that time on we needed to learn how to live with nature instead of following it. Consequently the Ego who followed nature became an almost obsolete part of the human body. Birds and animals migrate to other places according to nature's calling and directions. It was their egos that put them in motion.

Now that you, Soul, are in charge of your body, you don't need to follow the instructions of nature or your body's ego for your directions. You just need to rely on your Higher Self (HS) for help.

BLAMING EGO

When we ask ourselves what will make us happy, or into somebody, the reply may be, 'I don't know; I just don't know what to do or what to think.' That 'I don't know' means we as Soul, at some earlier time, have closed the communication link in our right brain which connected us to your Higher Self. We have closed the door in our head which connected us to the spirit realm. That means we are living from and relying on our left brain's reactive mind, which contains only our past experiences. This is the place where we view the movies of our early life.

We as Soul know we cannot learn anything from that place, yet we pass our responsibility for living over to that idiot called Ego, saying 'I think I will let Ego sort out for me what I want to do in the world. What do you think I should do, Ego?'

Wow! You have just put the cat amongst the pigeons. Ego has always wanted to be in charge of your life and you have just given it permission. Fancy asking a no-brainer like Ego to take charge of your life! What were we thinking about? Oh yes, sorry, I forgot. We weren't thinking. Ego doesn't have the ability to think, and that's most probably why we don't know what to do.

There is a twist in this little scenario. We already know that ego is as thick as two planks. All we are really doing here is refusing to take full responsibility for our actions. We love pointing our finger at anyone or anything when our life isn't working the way we want it to. In book 2 you will see how to take full responsibility for your actions, so this little get-out won't apply any more.

Tasks your body has learned to do are stored in a section of your mind that works on automatic. This saves you learning the same things over and over again. This gives you an opportunity to think of other things while creating an action.

Sometimes you suddenly go walkabout, which means you leave your body completely for a while. This leaves your body at the mercy of Ego. Ego panics first and then tries to takes control of the body. Ego remembers its instructions: 'You have only this life to live Ego, so ensure that Body survives.' Now Ego is only thinking of its own survival, but in its panic it is unsure what survival is, or what to do. So Ego uses the body's eyes to look around, hoping to find out what survival means. It comes up with the great idea that it means money, money and more money. After all, that's why we are here on Earth, isn't it? To be better than everyone else at making money and becoming rich, so we can have everything we want. So others can see how wealthy, how important, how brilliant we really are. So Ego reckons it's worked living out.

Then a voice from nowhere says: 'No Ego, that's not the truth, but it wasn't a bad effort for one incapable of thinking'.

Remember, Ego only knows how to react to things. It doesn't have the ability to think for itself, nor will it listen to or respect other people's points of view.

Take a look at this example and see if it reminds you of any people you have come across.

EGO GETS A JOB
(Honest – it's a fable).

So this little Ego upstart didn't listen to that remark above, and applied for a job it had lined up anyway and got it. The one thing Ego has is a knack of bragging about how good it is, and maybe it lies a little about what it can do. So it needs to form friendships with people who love to follow others, but don't ask questions about what they say.

They have to believe Ego's lies and think he is brilliant. So Ego makes many chosen friends, and his friends spread the lies/news around the firm on how brilliant he was. He looked at the salary of different department heads, and chose which one's money he would like to have.

He then used his guile to get that job, supported by his friends of course, even though they didn't really know what was going on. He worked his way up the firm's ladder until he became the manager of a section.

The way this Ego upstart got that manager sacked made the workers realise that he was ruthless, showed no mercy and had no respect for others. The sacked manager was a good caring manager, yet this little upstart had successfully got him sacked.

The workers didn't like the stories they heard about their new manager. He wouldn't listen to their complaints, and if they complained too often he would also sack them. They all began to live in fear of losing their jobs.

The boss's committee members noticed a decline in the firm's production, and started to frown and feel unhappy. They wanted to know the cause of this, so they went directly to the worker section and noticed glum, frowning faces, none of the laughing or joking that normally went on down there. They asked a few people what was wrong and nobody would say. Then one brave worker plucked up enough courage, and spilled the beans. He told them everything, right back to the time when he was the manager's best friend in the firm before he became manager.

Then he said: 'I'll most probably get the sack for telling you all this. That's the way it's been working around here since he became manager, but I feel so sorry for my friends here. I don't like seeing them working under threat. I don't like seeing them all miserable. This used to be a happy firm to work for, and it's breaking my heart the way it is right now. I would sooner be the one who has to leave than have them put up with this any more.'

The committee thanked him for being courageous enough to speak his mind and went back to discuss the matter with the boss. Later one of the committee members came back down and spoke to the one who had told the truth about what was going on, saying, 'You won't be losing your job, you think too much of your workmates for that to happen.' Instead, they sacked the Ego manager, and there is no prize for guessing which worker replaced him.

Some good had come to the new manager through that experience. Through being at one time friendly with that Ego upstart he had learned how to recognise deceit and lies. He had learned how to speak up for what he felt was right and he learned that he was not such a bad fellow after all. He is now glad to be who he is, doing what he does. And his workmates became like a second family to him.

His final words to the sacked manager were: 'I would like to thank you, little Ego upstart, for teaching me those things. I no longer need your help, and you are no longer welcome in my space. I will never forget you, and will be happy to love you for who you are, and for what you have taught me, but from a distance of course.'

So this little Ego upstart's life has suddenly come crashing down. He has fallen off his pedestal and landed where he really belongs, back on the ground, and it felt painful. Earth's energies have a knack of doing that to Egos who get it wrong big time. But knowing that doesn't help Ego's situation. Ego at the moment is too busy pointing the finger at those people it thinks ruined its life. It needs to get rid of more of the dark energy called 'rage' before it can calm down.

Soul was not impressed with that experience, and not impressed with the feelings its Body is having right now. When we try to live backwards, it causes mayhem in others, and in our own body. The cells in our body start deteriorating before their time is up. Just reverse the word 'LIVE' and come to your own conclusions about what was created in the above example.

Soul was wondering what had gone wrong. During this quiet time a different voice, much kinder than Ego's, spoke to him. 'I know you, you're my HS' said Soul. 'Where did I go wrong with my plan for fame?'

'You thought you were clever enough to have that experience without my assistance' replied HS. 'You decided to go it alone because you thought you knew it all. You thought you knew best, but you didn't, did you? You closed the door in your head, which broke your connection with me. Then you had only Earth's dark energies to work with. Not once did you open the door and ask for my advice until now, after the event. I tried to warn you many times, but you just refused to listen.

Even though you closed the door to me, I am still able to talk to you. But you pretended I wasn't there'.

Source deliberately created dark energies on earth, energies that are opposite to itself that is. Not with the intention of harming you, but to help you to stay on your true path of being loving.

HS (your knight in shining armour) is there to help you to stay loving in whatever you do or say. These dark energies are there to help you to learn how to respect and be considerate to your Body, to other Soul Beings and to Earth's nature. When you choose not to follow this request, when you choose to look on the dark side of things, or only at the things you personally want for yourself, this causes the cells in your Body to hurt a little. Your verbal or physical actions have hurt others *feelings,* and if you continue to show no respect to that person or situation, then the cells in your body will start hurting a lot more. If you refuse to change your mind about what you are saying, doing or thinking about life and others knowing your body is hurting, then you are causing your body to continue on a downward spiral until a full blown dis-ease appears. You flippantly call this 'getting sick'. Sometimes Earth claims back our Body.

Soul listened intently as HS continued its advice. 'The results of your experiences have nothing to do with me or Source' said HS. 'They are all created by you using your Free Will. Neither Source nor I have the power or right to do anything for you, like picking you up and putting you in another place away from the mess you have created. That would be breaking the rule we agreed on, of you being a god in your own right.

'We can help you however, by showing you ways of getting yourself out of any mess you put your body in. If you should accidentally get caught up in someone else's drama, or if there is nothing for you to learn from that experience, then we make sure you stay safe. You may call that a miracle. From your viewpoint, all we seem to do in the spirit realm is create miracles.

'Try keeping in communication with me and listen to the advice I offer you about your questions. Remember you are a god on Earth, so you have to make your own mind up about the choices I have to offer you.

'You are in charge of your body and its health. When you allow me to guide you, it becomes easier for you to choose the right path. Out of the ways I offer you, one way will cause all the cells in your body to smile and feel happy. That is the way your body feels it can create the action best.

'By listening to my options and choosing one, your life will start flowing better than you could ever imagine. It may even make you feel at times as if you are in heaven.

'My loving light energy is to give you good feelings to aim for, so remember to talk to me every time your world seems to get dark and pulls you down. Remember, you never stop learning. You are always at your wisest when your attention and awareness are in this present moment. From that point you can view all the pleasant and unpleasant things that are happening in your space, both in your body and in your outer environment as they happen.

'By staying in this Present moment (PT) it prevents your past experiences from affecting you, and taking you over. You need only move into your past to get something you want to correct or improve on.'

SUPERMARKET EXAMPLE

As you walk down the fruit section, your body's cells sense something that they need. Your eyes focus on the strawberries, and your body agrees they will do it good, so you instruct Ego to pick up a container, which it does.

Then your cells senses a mango that also has ingredients your body requires. Your cells went to ask you, but you weren't there, so they asked Ego to pick up a mango, but Ego refused. Why? Because in your mind that mango brought back to life the memories of a past experience where you disliked mangos (perhaps they fell off a lorry in front of you and damaged your car).

Ego doesn't care who tells it what to do, as long as it personally survives. Notice how quickly your cells asked Ego to do this action once they realised you had gone, and Ego went into your left mind to find out what to do and that mind took over. Your left mind is full of mixed-up disasters. No help ever comes from your mind.

Now, if you, Soul, were still there at the present time supervising the whole procedure, then Ego would have followed your command and picked up the mango, because Ego always trusts and follows your instructions. But unfortunately you weren't there at that moment in time; you had gone walkabout. You had just seen someone you might or might not have known, but fancied them like mad anyway. So you left what you were doing, in this case sorting out food to satisfy your body's needs, and disappeared into your imaginary world to create a make-believe experience with this fantastic person.

See! I told you, you often fly off without notice to be someplace else. The minute your disappearing act happened, negative beliefs started rising from your mind, and Ego followed their dictates.

I hope this example has given you some idea of what happens when you (Soul) play around with soul travelling at the wrong time. When you choose the wrong time to go walkabout your past, with the help of Ego, immediately comes to the surface and take over your life.

Now you know how fast things happen against your desire when you leave the only place you have to create an experience. I call that space Present Time (PT).

If you play this game too often, then you are spending too much time in your past, and it doesn't take long before your body starts feeling uncomfortable ill at ease.

Everything works in threes. Take one element away, and your life doesn't work properly. You, your ego and the cells in your body are the three energies that create all your experiences on Earth. Your skin is just its outer casing, but the expression on its face can speak volumes about its inner working.

Now let's see what happens when you give Ego a job it is suited to. Yes, Ego is good at doing some things and normally gets it right. But it's always in a hurry when doing things.

EMOTIONS

E = Energy, and energy is always in Motion. So E-motion is energy in motion = **Feelings**. An Emotional Feel prevents other energies from creating their actions.

When the cells in your body sense an Earth object, a thought or an unhealthy cell in its body, they pick up the vibration of that object. That object is resisting the flow of life force, and its energy vibration is creating a sensation in your body we call an *Emotion*. It is these disturbed cells in our body that create your feelings.

Your body is a fantastic feeling machine which you rely on to tell you how well it is doing when creating your actions. You, Soul, only know how to send out love. That is the only energy Source has, and you are made from the same substance as Source, so that is the only energy you have. Your HS talks to the cells in your body. This sets up a motion of *feelings,* for or against what it says. From this feeling we choose the best way to do something.

Oh dear, I have lots of bad memories! So not all my actions are created with love.

When you are being Soul, you project love into every cell in your body, and into every action you ask it to create. This allows others to know, through the energies your body sends out, just how much love you are projecting into the world. It is your body that tells the world how loving you are.

If this isn't the way it is in your life, then your body is suffering pain in some area of your body and your body is sending out a message to others that it is in pain. We all have the ability but only some people are able to sense that message.

Just look at the energy you receive from a new-born baby. Can you find anything there other than love? They are showing the same energy we have. We also brought love down to earth with us to use in our actions.

All other energies we use come from our resistance to love. Our body is an Earth object, and through its sensitivity we get to know about our resistive *feelings*. True love is the flow of pure energy. It has no Earth similarity. We cannot compare it to anything on earth. True love just IS.

All emotions, ranging from joy, false love and its marvellous pleasures right down to feeling completely useless, come from the resisting energies installed on Planet Earth by Source. They have been put here to help us to learn how not to be, and how not to do things.

HOW CELLS CREATE FEELINGS

Our cells form groups like little gangs. Some form the knee group, others the finger group, a part of the hand group. These groups link together to create our body. Their attention is more on the area they maintain than what the rest of the body is doing, yet they are always in touch with and affected by everything that happens in other parts of our body. They are always concerned about our body's overall health, even if it does not directly affect their department.

So all the cells are energy linked and form a team called your body. Each system works through its own channelled frequency. Each body system (and there are hundreds of them) such as your nervous system, blood system, digestive system etc, uses its own wavelength, just like a radio station. Each station on your inner radio system sends out its own information. When all your systems are working at peak condition, the end result is a healthy happy body with all cells smiling.

If there are any hold-ups or blocks in any of your body's circuits, then every cell knows about it in a fraction of a second. Any twinge, ache or slight pain is telling you, Soul, through *feelings* that something is getting out of balance in one of your body's systems. Either something physical is happening right now in the outside world, like you are sitting on a nail, or you may be looking at or listening to an angry person who is upsetting the cells in your body. Or your attention is on something in your left mind which is upsetting the cells in your body. In this case you are probably playing a re-run of some experience you had earlier in life, or re-running an imaginary experience that has never happened. The re-run of this upsetting situation is preventing a group of your cells from smiling, and you are feeling this in your body as an unpleasant emotional *feeling*.

An unpleasant feeling is caused by an action created without the flow of love attached, or inventing an action that does not contain love. If it is not flowing with love then it is flowing in the opposite direction. A reverse flow causes friction and friction causes *pain*, like that nail you were sitting on. Ouch, you felt that again didn't you? Isn't memory a wonderful thing?

OUR TWO UNIVERSES

The stars we see in the night sky are the end product of Source. The energy from their light arrives instantly, even though their light takes years to arrive on earth. They are the cells and organs forming the still-expanding body of Source.

That is as close as we will ever get to seeing Source. The planets and astrology signs we recognise in the heavens are sending their energies to Earth because Earth is one more cell in the Body of Sources. Both Earth and our bodies are affected by these energies. It doesn't matter if you believe in astrology or not, you are still affected by the energies in the body of Source.

The planet you do believe to have an effect on you is our sun - otherwise sun creams are a complete waste of time. All energies in space affect Earth's nature. They also affect our own personal inner universe.

Your body IS your personal universe. All energies affect your body, including those of other souls who have their attention on you and those souls who are in close range of your physical body.

Outside energies always affect you, but you are in charge of how outside energies are going to affect you. You have already created many beliefs and those beliefs act as your guidelines, or blockers on how you intend to use or not use the energies coming into your space right now.

The energy you receive from our sun helps you to put fire into your belly. The reflective energy you receive from our moon helps you to reflect on your day's activities. Evenings are a reflective time where you look back at the day just gone, and maybe at the next step you intend to take along your chosen path.

Our sun and moon are opposite, yet each has a good effect on our life depending on the way we use it. Both may cause you to feel pain, depending on the beliefs you are following or the actions you are creating at the time, and may show up as a loss to your comfort zone.

This also applies to all so-called Earth negative energies, eg if you lose your job, or something else you have become attached too. Suppose this something needed to be taken away from you before you became willing to move forward again. If you have a big ego you may even feel you are being forced to take your next step. But the choice is always yours. How gentle is gentle persuasion, and how much resistance do you wish to attach to it?

MENTALLY EXPERIENCING EMOTIONS

You need a body to sense the spiritual possibilities that appear in energy form. We often call that intuition, which really means inner-tuition.

When you put your attention on something, your body cells feels the energies attached to it. You, Soul, understand the emotion of your cells' energies, so you gain the knowledge of that which is being offered you. You call this recognising, gaining knowledge or becoming aware of something.

You have to put your attention on something before you can experience it mentally. If it's a solid object in this world you may touch it and feel its shape and texture. Your body cells feed you the information from that experience. Remember you only have the energy of love. It is your body that makes up its mind if it loves or dislikes what you are looking at or sensing, so it shows you an emotion somewhere between fun and fear according to the past beliefs it holds about that type of object. It always does this for survival of the body purposes.

It's as if you are asking your body: On a scale of 1 to 10

how do you feel about this material object you are looking at, or this mental image I have my attention on? Your body replies after looking at past beliefs it has made on that subject or item. Your cells are already feeling the pleasure or the pain of that past experience. If they say 'What you have your attention on is scaring me to death', then your body's cells will turn on its fight-or-flight system.

Every time you get your body to create an experience, your body is the effect of it and you are that much wiser. Your body forms an opinion which turns into a belief of like or dislike. Just imagine how many times your body does that action in the course of a day. Some of its beliefs are wrong, because of a lack of knowledge. No wonder our body is never happy for long - it is carrying too much rubbish around.

WHAT WE'VE LEARNED SO FAR

A part of Source volunteered to leave the womb of Source to experience living on Earth, so Source can experience Earth through its body's emotional and physical actions.

Source shook itself and millions of sparks flew out, known as Spirit Beings.

One of these Spirits gave birth to you, the Soul Being.

You know that Spirit as your Higher Self.

This makes you the Soul, a part of the Energy of Source.

You have access to all the knowledge Source has created via your Higher Self.

Your experiences pass on to Source automatically as you are a part of Source.

Source is able to experience Earth life vicariously through you and your body's emotions.

You, your body and HS work as a team.

When you go walkabout, the balance in your body is temporarily upset.

You, Soul, know there is an imbalance when you again tune into your body's feelings.

Now you know who you are it is much easier to make living on Earth more pleasurable.

Had you continued to believe that you 'have' a soul, you would never have found out who is in charge of your life. You would still believe you were something indefinably different, and as you have already found through living up to now, there is no way out of that mess.

Knowing who you really are should make you feel more comfortable about creating life.

You may feel more content in knowing you are something, or some-body.

By thinking you were, the body tricked you into believing that you needed to be controlled.

Your body is quite capable of doing some wonderful evil things when living backwards.

Now you have come home and stuck a label on yourself that clearly states, 'I Am Soul'.

Well done!

SOUL TRAVEL

Soul Travels to three destinations, believe it or not, and this may surprise you. You have been Soul travelling all your life.

Now you know that you own a body, you should realise that you live in and belong to three different worlds at the same time. Everything comes in threes.

DESTINATION 1 (POSSIBILITIES)

When you visit the right mind, you leave your body through the right brain and arrive at the world of images. Some call this your **imagination,** but this world is real because you left your body's world by an imaginary door in the right brain, and have arrived at the world of Source where everything IS the way it IS. This is also the place you meet and talk with your HS. The speed you travel there and back is so fast it may take less than a blink of an eye. It cannot be measured by Earth time. From this place your HS gives you the information you ask for.

DESTINATION 2 (PRESENT TIME)

In present time you put your attention on something or someone no matter how far away it is or they are. You instantly arrive there as Soul, looking at an *image* of the persons or the article.

As a Soul Being you have the ability to move from one room to the next by floating through walls and closed doors. How many times have you lost something, then got the impression it is in the other room. You actually went into that room as a Soul being and looked at it. We say 'I think it's in the other room'. There is nothing unusual, clever or painful in doing this, you have been doing it since the beginning of time. Sometimes if you are forgetful you may try walking through a closed door with your body, especially when your attention is in some other place. That experience is rather painful for your body. When you walked through a door without your body there was nothing to learn, but when you try to be clever and take your body with you, you soon find you have something to learn. Pain stimulates your desire to learn.

You quickly learn that earthly ways of travelling are different to spiritual ways of travelling.

You quickly learn that your earth body cannot do the same things you are capable of doing.

You learn that you have to follow Earth rules when using your body to create an experience.

Any discomfort felt by your body happens when you break either earth rules or spiritual rules or both. You would never try to create an experience of walking your body through a closed door if you loved and respected it. Your body is a very valuable piece of equipment. You use it to create your earth experiences, and you only get one per lifetime.

DESTINATION 3 (PAST CREATIONS)

The negative energies the cells in your body continuously record and store are so strong that at times they have the ability to drain your energy of love, so your left brain stores all this information in a space outside your body. This space we call your aura. It is the only mind your body has, and it is filled mostly with rubbish.

When we do something wrong and continually complain about it, all the energy connected to that experience and complaint goes into your body and to your left mind. We should be thinking about doing something to correct our mistake, but this mind does not allow that to happen. It's more of a finger-pointing energy, where we love to blame others for our mistakes.

Your personal Higher Self who dwells in destination 1 (the spirit realm) loves your body to bits, and most probably has a good laugh on the quiet at the antics you get your body to do at times. HS does its best to keep you on the right track with love, but we rarely listen. Nothing is ever done for you by spirit beings off their own backs, but they do give uplifting suggestions freely.

LOVE

Love is neither an emotion nor a feeling; Love Just IS. Love is YOU - Source and HS are also love. We are learning to act with love when we are not trying to be in any way an Earth-bound ego control freak. When we choose to act like an ego, we are supporting our mind's opinion of love.

MORE PROOF

I am about to ask you to do something you have been doing all your life, so this won't be hard for you. Read the next paragraph, then close your eyes and do as it asks.

Get a mental picture of someone you are happy with you know well. Look at their eyes, what do you see? Look at their clothes, what colours are they? What are they saying? Notice how they move around. Then open your eyes.

Did you notice how the images you created turned into a movie? They always do.

Your body's eyes were closed, so it wasn't your physical body looking at that movie. You, Soul, watched that movie, and your physical body always has a link to where you are - it's written in the contract - so it sensed the feelings coming from that person. You used what we call your sixth sense to see that person, and your sixth sense is You, plus you had help from your body cells' five senses to hear and bring the sounds into your body. These are the same tools you use when you use your imagination to assemble ideas you intend to create on earth.

The sixth sense is your ability to see things that come from the right mind. It's your ability to see those things that you have assembled but not created on Earth yet. Your body's five senses not only sense the end product of things. They also sense anything you are in the process of creating in the non-material universe that includes your dark thoughts.

You have always had the ability to perceive non-material images. But you need a body if you intend to tell somebody what you are looking at. They might think you are a bit mad, but that's OK; they never saw it, so it's not real for them anyway.

Is this making life more real for you? Can you see that you have more abilities than your body possesses? Do you now have sufficient proof that you are a powerful Soul Being who needs the use of a material body to make your dreams come true?

I do hope you are willing to take this belief on board and make it a part of your reality. Not because I said it, but because you have proved it for yourself to be your truth.

If it is now your truth, I dare you to make the following declaration truthfully:

'I know I am a Soul Being, I just travelled to a place without taking my body.'

Once you have accepted this reality you will agree that you are in charge of your body. Now you can play many different games to change the life you have with your body. And only you have the ability to make these changes. Soon you will knowingly be able to make life and living much more fun for yourself. Before you can do that however, there is a little more for you to know.

OUR TWO REALITIES

From the beliefs we make and the experiences we create, we form our reality of life. As a baby you were living 100% as a Soul Being. Your energies were pure love and you could not do anything wrong. You may have had what earth beings call 'imaginary friends'. They weren't imaginary from your point of view, they were real, and that was the way it was supposed to be. They were there helping you through your early years. You are never here on your own.

When you reached the age of six or maybe eight, some older children may have made fun of you, laughed at you and called you names. These were the ones who no longer believe in Father Christmas. They were getting into a newly-forming belief given to them by their elders that reality can only be found on Earth.

If you didn't like hearing what those children said about

you, it upset you and made you feel different to the rest of the kids. So you decided to do what they were telling you to do, to 'grow up'. This meant getting rid of your imaginary friends.

That task was easier said than done. Your imaginary friends kept coming back; they couldn't understand why you didn't love them any more or why you didn't want to see them. Eventually you won the day. You found a way to block or trick them out of your life, and they were gone forever.

When you closed the door to your spirit friends, you also closed the door to your HS and the spirit realm. You then put your full attention on the real business of learning how to live on Earth. Unknown to you at the time, this was your first step in creating a downward spiral of living. When you try to do everything on your own without your Higher Self's help, you fall into the energy traps of your left mind, because that is the only mind you have.

The energy in the spirit realm lifts you up, the energies in this material world pull you down.

You are still able to hear the communications directed to you from your HS, if you cared to listen that is. But you most probably justified this by saying it was only your imaginary friends trying to come through again, or you thought those sounds were just more ego chatter.

All you have now to gain knowledge and awareness about living on Earth is your body's five sensing mechanisms. You rely only on the objects you see on Earth and on the things others tell you. This is all you have left to try and make sense of living life on Earth.

This allows others to control you more easily. Anyone who

you think has more knowledge than you have, you tend to worship. Often you accept their beliefs without even giving them another thought, and you follow their desires as if they are God's gift to you. Slowly, as a non-thinking being, you fall deeper into your left mind's traps.

As you may notice, we have many zombies walking the Earth instead of loving Soul Beings. There are still lots of thinking Souls creating their lives, but few know who they are. Fewer know they are connected to Source, and fewer still are living in harmony with all there is.

We say: 'No I am not dreaming. No I'm not living in a fantasy world'. Oh dear! What a pity! That's the only real world there is. Where else are you going to get ideas that increase your awareness and give you knowledge?

Many people don't realise that every materialised construction or object in this world is the end result of somebody's fantasy, somebody's dream creation. They had a strong desire to create that object on Earth. All Earth objects are the end product, the end result of somebody's dream. To create that dream, they had to go into their *right brain*, to make contact with their HS, who went into the Source of All there Is and brought out the moving images that helped them to gain the knowledge on how to create that dream. Then they brought those images down to Earth as knowledge and got their body to create that dream.

Some people kept their spirit friends but never talked about them, for fear of being ridiculed, or considered weird. When they get older they learn that the world does accept some spirit communications, as long as the spirit has an acceptable name.

113

We usually find these names in our historical and religious books. Those names are acceptable because they are believed to be 'Greater Beings'.

I am not criticizing anyone who works with spirits in any shape or form. They are all doing a good job by keeping the door to the spirit realm open. They are preventing us from becoming 100% Earth-bound zombies. So I thank you all for the work you are doing, from the bottom of my heart.

Sometimes our ego puts a name to our spirit guide to make us appear important.

Why do we have to attach a name to a spirit energy we sense and do not see? We should be interested in the information it gives, not its name.

We may believe that quoting a well-known name makes the subject matter more truthful. Sometimes we invent the whole scenario ourselves and believe it came to us from above. That is why unnamed Souls with a body are often mistakenly recognised as being the name which has been given to their body by their parents. You are really a No-body.

Remember, this book is my point of view, which is different from that of other beings. I know this, and this is my truth. It's not a question of who is right or who is wrong. This is just another way you can try to see if you can learn something about life and about your true Self.

When we become Earth bound, we rely only on our *left mind*, which holds the record of our past. We spend most of our time looking at *past* experiences that went wrong. I call this our Ego mind, but that is not really fair as it suggests a dislike for Ego. It also means we are blaming Ego for everything that goes wrong in our life. Our Ego doesn't have the sense to know what is right or wrong or what's going on in the world. Ego is just a vibrating energy unit, doing its best to create actions that keep it alive. Its only real interest is in the survival of your body, because that's where it lives.

MIND WHAT YOU SAY, AND EMPTY WORDS

I often record my sessions so clients have a record of what we have achieved. When they listening to the recording their imaginations kick in and they gain a better reality about their session. Recording has been a big learning curve for me. When I started recording I was disgusted with the way I said things. It felt as if another person was speaking, not me. At times it showed bluntness with a demanding attitude which I didn't know existed in me, and other faults I knew about came in - my ego was having a field day. I just couldn't believe it was me saying things that way or with that tone of voice.

I still learn from my present recording. My approach has improved over 20-odd years, but as my awareness lifts there is always more for me to learn. I learned that I make my biggest mistakes when I get distracted and fall out of the moment and into the world around me, or into my left mind for a while.

We often drop out of Present Time when we are interrupted from what we are doing, or we find it difficult to accept what another just said. We should stay in PT and keep calm, but if we were not pleased about being interrupted or about what they just said then we often run to our mind to find a quick reply. This is known as reacting, and normally it isn't very loving. Then we blame our Ego for the thing we come out with.

The truth is we often chose to go into our mind to solve problems. We believe Earth and our mind are the only reality we have, and by making that choice we fall into our past mistakes and our past way of doing things.

Our mind contains nothing which will connect us to our future intentions.

We may say 'If I can't hear it then it doesn't exist. If I can't see it then it's not real'. They are our deep down blocking beliefs that are preventing us from learning truths. Can you remember where you came from? We need to get back into the right mind in order to live life in a more fulfilling way.

Our body's mind has learned some fancy phrases, like 'I love you'. But that mind doesn't really know what love means, so we cannot put the *feelings* of that energy into practice.

At times I overhear lovers' tiffs and hear them saying those magic words, 'I love you' as they part company with rage on their faces. Which one of them was demonstrating love I haven't a clue.

And how about the latest traditional greeting: 'Peace, love, and light'. Nice words mate, but what does it mean? It's as if half the sentence is missing. Are they receiving it from me, giving it to me or just saying it because it sounds like a nice thing to say?

'Have you just done something to me?' That is the question I often want to ask them. Only rarely do I feel those energies arrive in my body from someone. If you like saying these sweet things, then mean what you say by creating that energy's action. Make sure you are sending your love energies (that is the action) for those words to the person you are saying them to, so their body cells know they are truly receiving loving energy from you.

If I was in a pub and somebody said to me 'love and light' I would say: 'Sorry mate, I prefer the dark, I find it a much tastier beer'.

What I am really trying to put over here is: Now that you know who you are, you need to get to know yourself better by getting into the moment. Relax your body and then you will *think more clearly about what you want to say before you speak*. You will then mean every word you say.

One way to get to know your 'self' is to use a recorder and listen to how others hear you coming across. You will soon find out how your true nature sounds. Do you sound loving, egoistic or maybe a little forceful, or, are you pretending you are not there by speaking so quietly?

Never tell yourself off. Always do the best you can, all the time. It is OK to laugh at your errors - then the dark energies will not stick to your cells and cause your body problems.

Now is the time to set the books right about your God.

When was the last time God did something for you, something you never created on Earth yourself? We have to be careful when answering this question because we create both physically and mentally. Mentally, anything we put our attention on, we may attract into our life. That is the energy of the Law of Attraction working for us. This law is similar to the law of gravity – jump up and you will come down. Neither of these is God doing something for us, or to us.

THE PISCEAN AGE CAUSED US PROBLEMS

We may have misunderstood the true meaning of the Pisces sign. The fish were looking both ways. The sign was saying, look carefully at the opposite point of view before making any decisions. We never understood that message.

We *thought* two fish swimming in the opposite direction meant we had to learn how to separate from each other, to split up so we wouldn't live as a loving human race. Over the centuries our mistakes have taught us how not to live on Earth, and that's a good thing.

Maybe we needed to know how it felt to get everything wrong for a special reason. We learned that trying to be a bigger god than Source didn't work. We learned that relying on our mind for answers doesn't solve any of our problems.

I have learned that, and that is why I am writing this book. Most of our problems are 'mental images' and need to be thought through using our right brain, and *right mind*. They cannot be solved by going inwards and using our body's left brain mind, or by looking at Earth's material world of finished articles.

If you are not too sure about any of the above, then take another look at what is not working in your life and ask yourself - where did you get that information from? Did you tune into your right brain and go out the door to the right mind?

Look around you and accept the truth of what you see. Just *be* there and observe for a while, with no judging, justifying or finger pointing. Can you see how we have nearly ruined our Earth's playground? How did we do that so successfully? We have all played our part in making the world the way it is. Even friends sometimes become our enemies, as we feel when our partner relationship goes wrong.

TAILPIECE

You have now learned who you are and know who is in charge of your life. You could see how easy it was, when you did not know who you were, to be led along non-survival paths of ups and down where the ups came to a sudden end and the downs took you deeper than where you started. Some of us learned to follow others, but a threat of losing our job if we did not comply by their rules did not please us. A loss of job may also lead to a loss of car, house etc. There is no way up by moving along those paths, only more misery.

That controlling way of life was set in motion by our ancestors and needs to be brought to an end.

Over the past few thousand years we have learned what *not* to do.

Now we know who we are, we need to learn what we *can* do and how to apply it on Earth.

It is up to you to learn how to create your own experiences the way you intended to before you came to Earth. Remember - you are never alone.

Book 2 shows you how to use the tools you possess to make your desires become a reality.

Some of your tools may be a little rusty through lack of use. Some may need repairing.

So let's get started and put the *Wow Energy* back into your life.oth

www.ingramcontent.com/pod-product-compliance
Lightning Source LLC
Chambersburg PA
CBHW060312050426
42448CB00009B/1803